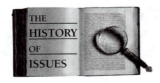

THE
HISTORY
OF
ISSUES

Gun Control

Other Books in the History of Issues Series:

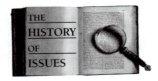

THE
HISTORY
OF
ISSUES

Gun Control

Mitchell Young, Book Editor

GREENHAVEN PRESS

An imprint of Thomson Gale, a part of The Thomson Corporation

THOMSON

GALE

Detroit • New York • San Francisco • New Haven, Conn. • Waterville, Maine • London

Christine Nasso, *Publisher*
Elizabeth Des Chenes, *Managing Editor*

© 2007 Thomson Gale, a part of The Thomson Corporation.

Thomson and Star logo are trademarks and Gale and Greenhaven Press are registered trademarks used herein under license.

For more information, contact:
Greenhaven Press
27500 Drake Rd.
Farmington Hills, MI 48331-3535
Or you can visit our Internet site at http://www.gale.com

LIBRARY OF CONGRESS CATALOGING-IN-PUBLICATION DATA

Gun control / Mitchell Young, book editor.
    p. cm. -- (History of issues)
    Includes bibliographical references and index.
    ISBN-13: 978-0-7377-2003-7 (hardcover : alk. paper)
    ISBN-10: 0-7377-2003-4 (hardcover : alk. paper)
    1. Gun control--United States. 2. Firearms ownership--United States. I. Young, Mitchell.
    HV7436.G8673 2007
    363.330973--dc22
                                                        2006021349

Printed in the United States of America
10 9 8 7 6 5 4 3 2 1

Contents

Chapter 1: Guns in Early America

Chapter 2: Debating the Purpose of the Second Amendment

Chapter 5: Gun Control Issues and Activism

Foreword

In the 1940s, at the height of the Holocaust, Jews struggled to create a nation of their own in Palestine, a region of the Middle East that at the time was controlled by Britain. The British had placed limits on Jewish immigration to Palestine, hampering efforts to provide refuge to Jews fleeing the Holocaust. In response to this and other British policies, an underground Jewish resistance group called Irgun began carrying out terrorist attacks against British targets in Palestine, including immigration, intelligence, and police offices. Most famously, the group bombed the King David Hotel in Jerusalem, the site of a British military headquarters. Although the British were warned well in advance of the attack, they failed to evacuate the building. As a result, ninety-one people were killed (including fifteen Jews) and forty-five were injured.

Early in the twentieth century, Ireland, which had long been under British rule, was split into two countries. The south, populated mostly by Catholics, eventually achieved independence and became the Republic of Ireland. Northern Ireland, mostly Protestant, remained under British control. Catholics in both the north and south opposed British control of the north, and the Irish Republican Army (IRA) sought unification of Ireland as an independent nation. In 1969, the IRA split into two factions. A new radical wing, the Provisional IRA, was created and soon undertook numerous terrorist bombings and killings throughout Northern Ireland, the Republic of Ireland, and even in England. One of its most notorious attacks was the 1974 bombing of a Birmingham, England, bar that killed nineteen people.

In the mid-1990s, an Islamic terrorist group called al Qaeda began carrying out terrorist attacks against American targets overseas. In communications to the media, the organization listed several complaints against the United States. It generally opposed all U.S. involvement and presence in the Middle East. It particularly objected to the presence of U.S. troops in Saudi Arabia, which is the home of several Islamic holy sites. And it strongly condemned the United States for supporting the nation of Israel, which it claimed was an oppressor of Muslims. In 1998 al Qaeda's leaders issued a fatwa (a religious legal statement) calling for Muslims to kill Americans. Al Qaeda acted on this order many times—most memorably on September 11, 2001, when it attacked the World Trade Center and the Pentagon, killing nearly three thousand people.

These three groups—Irgun, the Provisional IRA, and al Qaeda—have achieved varied results. Irgun's terror campaign contributed to Britain's decision to pull out of Palestine and to support the creation of Israel in 1948. The Provisional IRA's tactics kept pressure on the British, but they also alienated many would-be supporters of independence for Northern Ireland. Al Qaeda's attacks provoked a strong U.S. military response but did not lessen America's involvement in the Middle East nor weaken its support of Israel. Despite these different results, the means and goals of these groups were similar. Although they emerged in different parts of the world during different eras and in support of different causes, all three had one thing in common: They all used clandestine violence to undermine a government they deemed oppressive or illegitimate.

The destruction of oppressive governments is not the only goal of terrorism. For example, terror is also used to minimize dissent in totalitarian regimes and to promote extreme ideologies. However, throughout history the motivations of terrorists have been remarkably similar, proving the old adage that "the more things change, the more they remain the same." Arguments for and against terrorism thus boil down to the same set of universal arguments regardless of the age: Some argue that terrorism is justified to change (or, in the case of state terror, to maintain) the prevailing political order; others respond that terrorism is inhumane and unacceptable under any circumstances. These basic views transcend time and place.

Similar fundamental arguments apply to other controversial social issues. For instance, arguments over the death penalty have always featured competing views of justice. Scholars cite biblical texts to claim that a person who takes a life must forfeit his or her life, while others cite religious doctrine to support their view that only God can take a human life. These arguments have remained essentially the same throughout the centuries. Likewise, the debate over euthanasia has persisted throughout the history of Western civilization. Supporters argue that it is compassionate to end the suffering of the dying by hastening their impending death; opponents insist that it is society's duty to make the dying as comfortable as possible as death takes its natural course.

Greenhaven Press's The History of Issues series illustrates this constancy of arguments surrounding major social issues. Each volume in the series focuses on one issue—including terrorism, the death penalty, and euthanasia—and examines how the debates have both evolved and remained essentially the same over the years. Primary documents such as newspaper articles, speeches, and government reports illuminate historical developments and offer perspectives from throughout history. Secondary sources provide overviews and commentaries from a more contemporary perspective. An introduction begins each anthology and supplies essential context and background. An annotated table of contents, chronology, and index allow for easy reference, and a bibliography and list of organizations to contact point to additional sources of information on the book's topic. With these features, The History of Issues series permits readers to glimpse both the historical and contemporary dimensions of humanity's most pressing and controversial social issues.

Introduction

"A well regulated Militia, being necessary to the security of a free State, the right of the people to keep and bear Arms, shall not be infringed." That statement, the Second Amendment to the United States Constitution, is at the heart of the fierce debate over gun control. A fundamental argument exists over the nature of the right enshrined in the amendment. Gun rights supporters see it as guaranteeing the right of individuals to own guns free of government control. Gun control advocates, on the other hand, believe the amendment was written to guarantee the right to own guns for participation in state-organized military units such as the National Guard. These two perspectives are often referred to, respectively, as the individual right view and the collective right view.

The confusion over the exact meaning of the Second Amendment is rooted in its history. The American right to bear arms evolved from English law. Most American colonial leaders were of British descent and were naturally influenced by English customs. When devising the Constitution and Bill of Rights, the newly independent Americans turned to English tradition for inspiration. One of the most important influences was the English Bill of Rights, which stated that "Protestants may have arms for their defence suitable to their conditions and as allowed by law."

The right to bear arms was important to the English for two reasons: Firearms allowed for self-defense against common criminality, and they were necessary to protect Englishmen's liberties against government oppression. Like their English predecessors, the framers of the United States Constitution saw firearms as the ultimate protection from governmental tyranny. Seeking to ease fears that the new federal government and its army would be an oppressive power,

James Madison wrote in *Federalist 46*, "To [the federal army] would be opposed a militia amounting to near half a million of citizens with arms in their hands, officered by men chosen from among themselves, fighting for their common liberties, and united and conducted by governments possessing their affections and confidence." Madison foresaw a nation in which most adult males were potential members of a militia to oppose federal tyranny. As such, they had a right to bear arms to protect their personal liberty and their community against tyrannical government.

Gun rights advocates point to this history to support their view that gun ownership is an individual right. Since all adult males were potential militia members, it stands to reason that all adult males—as individuals—had the right to bear arms. Furthermore, they argue, it makes no sense to claim that the government can regulate weapons that are intended to serve as a check against oppression by the very same government. Therefore, efforts to control guns are unconstitutional.

Gun control advocates dismiss this argument. They insist that militia members had the right to own guns only to the extent that they were needed for militia service. Thus gun ownership was not an individual right, but a collective right subject to government regulation. Consequently, gun control laws are constitutional.

A History of Gun Control

Not long after the founding of the United States, the realities of trying to create a new, civilized society eclipsed the concern over governmental tyranny. In 1813 Kentucky passed a law prohibiting concealed weapons in an attempt to cut down on escalating violence in frontier towns. The state legislature did not, however, try to take away rifles—the sort of weapon useful for militia service. Other state legislatures followed Kentucky's lead; by 1850, every state west of the Appalachians had a law restricting the carrying of concealed weapons, and the courts upheld most of these restrictions.

Further gun control measures were enacted following the Civil War (1861–1865). The societal turbulence created by the war had made firearms easy to obtain, leading to the emergence of numerous private armed militias. State governments sought to crack down on these militias by passing laws against them. In Illinois, one such law was tested in a case that reached the U.S. Supreme Court. In *Presser v. Illinois* (1886), the Court ruled that the right to bear arms did not include the right to organize a paramilitary unit. The right to bear arms in a militia applied only to state-sponsored units. However, Justice William Woods, writing for the Court, also said that states could not prohibit weapons possession because "the States cannot . . . prohibit the people from keeping and bearing arms, so as to deprive the United States of their rightful resource for maintaining the public security." In sum, the Court allowed states to regulate guns but not to entirely ban them.

The next major gun control controversy arose in the 1930s. The growth of organized crime during the Prohibition era of the previous decade, as well as a more activist role for the federal government under President Franklin Roosevelt, led to a demand for gun control. In 1934 Congress passed the National Firearms Act, which was primarily focused on controlling the types of weapons used by gangsters as well as the transport of weapons across state lines. Later legislation, the 1938 Federal Firearms Act, created a national licensing system for gun dealers and importers.

These new laws caused a renewed controversy over the meaning of the Second Amendment. Two men convicted under the 1934 National Firearms Act for transporting a sawed-off shotgun across state lines challenged their conviction on the basis of their Second Amendment right to keep and bear arms. In *United States v. Miller* (1939), the U.S. Supreme Court ruled that the government was permitted to regulate or even ban firearms that were not "part of the ordinary military equipment" or that could not "contribute to the common defense." In other words, the right to bear arms applied only to those enrolled in state-organized militias; it was a collective right that was subject to regulation by the government. *Miller* led to a string of court rulings in favor of government's right to control weapons.

The successful regulations of the 1930s set the stage for the next wave of gun control laws beginning in the 1960s. That decade saw a dramatic rise in crime. In response, Congress passed the Gun Control Act of 1968, which prohibited the selling of guns to convicted criminals, mental patients, and drug users. Its enforcement mechanism was weak, however, as the law relied on the gun purchaser to be truthful on the form required for a gun purchase. Gun control was strengthened when in 1993 the Brady Handgun Violence Prevention Act was enacted by Congress. The act required a mandatory waiting period for gun purchases and instituted a nationwide criminal background check system. The same year, the Violent Crime Control and Law Enforcement Act banned certain types of military-style assault weapons. None of these laws was overturned on constitutional grounds because the courts had repeatedly held that the right to bear arms applied only to militias or to what is considered today's equivalent of militias, state National Guard units.

Resurgence of the Individual Right View

The position that the Second Amendment bestows a right to possess firearms only in connection with state militia service is still the prevailing legal opinion in the country. However, that view is coming under fire from legal scholars and historians. Sanford Levinson, a Texas law professor, has investigated the language of the Second Amendment as well as the concept of the colonial militia. He has come to the conclusion that the right to participate in the militia—and thus to be armed—was very broad; it did not apply only to state organized units. Thus, he favors the individual right interpretation. Historian

Joyce Lee Malcolm has studied the origins of the Second Amendment in English law. She has concluded that it was fear that the militia system could be used by government as an instrument of oppression that led to the English right of all Protestant subjects to possess weapons. Only an armed people could be an effective force against the infringement of liberty. Thus the right to bear arms must be free of governmental control. This idea was adopted by the framers of the Constitution when they drew up the Second Amendment, according to Malcolm.

This trend back to the individual right view of the Second Amendment began in the late 1990s and early 2000s. The pattern seems to be that the individual right view prevails during eras of conservative government, while the collective right view dominates during periods of more liberal government as in the 1930s and 1960s. No doubt the pendulum will swing back once again to the collective right view. As long as the United States exists, it is likely that partisans will argue over whether the Second Amendment applies to all individuals or only to those who participate in state militias.

THE
HISTORY
OF
ISSUES

Guns in Early America

Chapter Preface

America is often said to have a gun culture. This statement has two meanings. First, gun ownership—and gun use—are more common in the United States than elsewhere. Second, Americans have developed a strong attachment to firearms as part of their national culture. Yet these strong feelings about firearms have not stopped legislators from trying to regulate how people use them. This chapter focuses on the historical roots of the national attitude toward guns. In particular it deals with the concept of "the militia," the idea of the frontier, and the desire of states and localities to control gun use and gun violence in their territories.

The American gun culture goes back to the colonial era. The mostly English settlers who founded the original colonies brought with them ideas about firearms. The right and duty of the English to own and train with weapons—first with the longbow, later with firearms—was a source of pride in England. Starting in the Middle Ages, able-bodied males in towns and villages were organized into militias that served to defend their homes, their communities, and even the entire kingdom. The English settlers on America's eastern seaboard brought both their habit of participating in militias and the philosophy of an "armed people" that went along with this type of military organization.

The militia as a communal organization undoubtedly shaped the views of early American statesmen like James Madison and Thomas Jefferson. However, early America also gave rise to a strong individualist tradition of the lone frontiersman making his way in the wilderness with the help of his rifle. James Fenimore Cooper's novel *The Last of the Mohicans* is an example of this ideal. Natty Bumppo, Cooper's hero, is an expert marksman; his skill with his long rifle frequently saves his life. As America expanded westward, this ideal was reinforced by thousands of pioneer families who relied to some extent on firearms for protection and for hunting food.

Ironically, it was in just these frontier areas that the first calls for gun control arose. The frontier state of Kentucky, in 1813, was the first to pass a statewide limitation on guns. The legislature targeted concealed weapons in an attempt to control the violence that plagued its new settlements. Arkansas, another frontier state, passed a similar law about twenty years after Kentucky. In the West, it was common for towns to have local laws forbidding the carrying of weapons. Cowboys and farmers visiting these towns were required to check their weapons with the local sheriff and collect them again on the way out of town.

While the frontier has long since passed into history, the American ideal of self-reliance and self-defense lives on in the gun owners who claim the right to defend themselves with their own weapons. Another American tradition, started by the Kentucky legislature almost two centuries ago, of trying to limit gun rights in order to control gun violence also continues to find advocates among the public and policy makers.

The English Origins of Gun Rights

Joyce Lee Malcolm

The settlers in the original American colonies were deeply influenced by English traditions. One of those traditions was English citizens' obligation to defend their home, community, and country. In this article Joyce Lee Malcolm, an expert in English legal history, shows how the English, from small farmers to large landowners, fulfilled their obligation by serving in a local militia.

Militia members were expected to serve when called upon by local officials to quell disturbances. They were also obliged to serve the king in case of foreign invasion or internal rebellion. These requirements applied to almost all levels of English society. Simple farmers provided their own weapons and equipment and were required to keep up their skill in the use of these weapons—at first the longbow and later the firearm—through regular target practice. English citizens therefore needed to own their own bows or guns.

The English often resented militia duty because of the time required for training and service, but the ability to carry weapons and defend their own community was also a source of pride. These rights and attitudes would cross the Atlantic with the settlement of the English in North America.

The right of citizens to be armed not only is unusual, but evolved in England in an unusual manner: it began as a duty. From the proverbial "time out of mind" Englishmen had a duty to be armed. Like most duties it was often resented and, in this instance, commonly regarded as onerous, if not dangerous. Yet, at a crucial moment in English history, when

Joyce Lee Malcolm, *To Keep and Bear Arms: The Origins of an Anglo-American Right*. Cambridge, MA: Harvard University Press, 1994, pp. 1–6. Copyright © 1994 by the president and fellows of Harvard College. All rights reserved. Reproduced by permission of Harvard University Press.

the governing classes seized a rare opportunity to draw up a bill of rights, this long-standing and unpopular duty was transformed into a right. Its development as a duty was quite natural, as a right far more complex.

Citizen-Soldiers

The decentralization and disorder of the Middle Ages made popular participation in local peacekeeping the most practical means of maintaining order. The authority of the Crown [i.e., the king or queen] had increased substantially by the sixteenth and seventeenth centuries, but its limited financial resources led to the continuation of a practice that had, among other benefits, the virtue of being cheap. Similarly, the difficulty and expense of maintaining permanent armies and [the] popular hatred of mercenaries compelled the Crown to rely instead upon citizen-soldiers to defend the realm. Both policies involved considerable risk, since English subjects would have to be armed and trained to arms. What surprises is not the use of these medieval expedients, but their persistence into modern times—that the arms pressed into the hands of the general population as the most practical means of ensuring public quiet remained there. Indeed, the Crown's attempt late in the seventeenth century to shift to less perilous methods of maintaining order provoked the political nation to claim for all Protestants a right to have weapons. That right played a major role in the evolution of limited government.

It was during the seventeenth century that this transformation of a duty to have arms into a right took place. To understand why it occurred then, indeed why it occurred at all, we must focus upon that pivotal era. The seventeenth century is deservedly famous for its periodic and unprecedented political turmoil. It was a time of urgent concern with the boundaries of subjection and sovereignty and the obligations of government and religion. Yet the setting in which most Englishmen lived and worked remained in many respects unchanged by the upheavals in church and state. England was, and remained, overwhelmingly rural, with most of its people clustered in small villages of less than 500 persons. It was a society dominated by a landed aristocracy but comprising many prosperous independent farmers—England's famed yeomen—and increasing numbers of merchants, professionals, and craftsmen, the "middling sort." The great majority of Englishmen, however, were small freeholders or tenant farmers. Although civil war would loosen the aristocracy's grip on power, they dominated Parliament at the end of the century as they had at its start.[1] With the exception of the Civil War years, ordinary Englishmen were not noticeably more enthusiastic about their police duties in 1689 [when the English Bill of Rights was adopted] than in 1600. But against this background of sameness was a foreground of turmoil in which a man's ability to have weapons assumed grave significance. Before investigating the complex forces that would produce this transformation, one must examine the Englishman's traditional role as peacekeeper.

Englishmen Protect Themselves from Crime

England would not have a standing army until late in the seventeenth century, or a professional police force until the nineteenth century. From "time out of mind," therefore, the Englishman had been obliged to add to his other civic duties the dangerous chore of law enforcement. His first responsibility was to defend himself. He was also expected to protect his family and his property against attack. It was assumed he would have the means at hand to do this, and he was held legally blameless for any harm inflicted upon his assailants. As a popular seventeenth-century guidebook for justices of the peace [local judges] explained: "If Thieves shall come to a Man's House, to rob or murther [murder] him, he may lawfully assemble company to defend his House by force; and if

---

1. The English Civil War was waged from 1625 to 1649.

he or any of his company shall kill any of them in defence of Himself, his Family, his Goods or House, This is no Felony, neither shall they forfeit any thing therefore."

It is natural to expect a man to defend himself and his loved ones, but the Englishman was obliged to protect his neighbour as well. From at least the early Middle Ages, whenever a serious crime occurred villagers, "ready apparelled," were to raise a "hue and cry" and, under the supervision of the local constable or sheriff, pursue the culprit "from town to town, and from county to county" on "pain of grievous fine [Parliamentary writ of 1252]." In addition, the law made residents of a parish liable for compensating a victim of a robbery or riot committed in their parish for half of his loss. The development of firearms made the pursuit of culprits an increasingly dangerous obligation. Late in the seventeenth century—a heyday of highway robbers—Parliament attempted to modify collective responsibility. . . . But the bill failed and the obligation remained.

Another police duty placed upon the people was the keeping of watch and ward. Town gates were closed from sundown until sunrise, and each householder was required to take his turn keeping watch at night or ward during the day. The watch was to be carried out "by men able of body, and sufficiently weaponed [according to the Statute of Winchester (1285)]." Widows and householders of unsound body had to hire a substitute. During times of war or unrest the number of watchers was usually doubled. Anyone who failed to stand watch was liable to be put in the stocks or presented at quarter sessions [quarterly court hearings]. As in the case of hue and cry, the obligation caused concern and even resistance by the second half of the seventeenth century. Growing numbers of men and women from all classes were cited for refusal to perform their duty.

Beyond the local peacekeeping tasks of "hue and cry" and "watch and ward," all able-bodied men were bound to help the sheriff put down riots as members of his *posse comitatus*. By the seventeenth century the trained bands of the militia were generally summoned for this task, but the duty to serve on a posse continued, and posses were not uncommon during the Civil War.

Militia Service Required of All Men

A man's civic responsibility to help keep the peace stretched beyond his village and even beyond his county. He owed his sovereign [king] service in the militia. Such service was a source of both pride and vexation. The English liked to boast that they were [in the words of English political leader Oliver Cromwell] "the freest subjects under Heaven" because, among other things, they had the right "to be guarded and defended from all Violence and Force, by their own Arms, kept in their own hands, and used at their own charge under their Prince's Conduct".

Of course, they were seldom actually pleased at having to serve in the militia, and to do so at their own charge, but militia service appears to have been an integral part of English life from early times. With the exception of the first years of Norman rule, Anglo-Saxon, Norman, Angevin, Lancastrian, and Tudor kings chose to trust their subjects with arms and to modify and supplement the militia if need be, rather than to abolish it. So keen were monarchs to develop a citizen-army that by 1252 not only freemen but the richer villeins [serfs] were ordered to be armed, and in the years that followed unfree peasants were included as well. "The state in its exactions," [British historian] F. W. Maitland wrote, "pays little heed to the line between free and bond, it expects all men, not merely all freemen, to have arms." These acts formed the basis for Edward I's great Statute of Winchester of 1285, which organized the military might of the realm. For much of English history, therefore, the emphasis was on extending and fixing the obligation to keep and supply militia weapons, not disarming Englishmen. It was not who was supposed to be armed, but who was to pay for the arms, and where subjects were bound to battle, that became the chief sources of contention by the seventeenth century.

All able-bodied men between the ages of sixteen and sixty were liable for militia service, but from 1573 it had become the practice to select small groups of men, commonly known as trained bands, for special training. Such service was not popular, and the duty tended to devolve upon the poorer farmers and less prosperous craftsmen. During the seventeenth century at least 90,000 men served in the trained bands of England and Wales at any one time.

The militia was financed by a tax levied on anyone with any income, even the clergy and the poor. Poor men were usually grouped in such a way that several families might be jointly responsible for "finding" a single piece of military equipment, whereas, at the opposite end of the economic scale, a wealthy landowner might be responsible for producing a mounted man fully equipped, complete with pay in his pocket to last him some thirty days. Although the clergy contributed to the militia, they were not expected to fight. After the English Reformation Catholics were in a similar position, expected to contribute but not to participate. Unlike their fellow subjects, Catholics were not allowed to keep their militia weapons at home.

Militias Were a Defensive Force

This seventeenth-century militia was not the flexible force English kings of the time required. A thicket of obligations and customs spelled out each county's military duties and the use the king might make of its militia. The militia was first and foremost a defensive force and could not be taken out of the realm [kingdom]. Members were even reluctant to leave their own counties. As commander-in-chief of the militia the king decided when to call out the trained bands and what their task was to be. However, it was the local magnates—lords lieutenant, deputy-lieutenants, and lower-ranking officers—who were responsible for carrying out royal orders. Their power to interpret or misinterpret royal wishes should not be underestimated. For their part, rank-and-file militiamen were unreliable when called upon to put down internal riots whenever their sympathies lay with the rioters.

The militia, therefore, could serve to some extent as the king's hammer against either an invader or the great magnates, and an inexpensive hammer at that, but it afforded both the aristocracy and ordinary subjects some control over royal policy. And, of course, it necessitated the arming and training of a very large portion of the population.

With the development during the seventeenth century of professional, well-drilled armies on the Continent, English kings were tempted to abandon the militia in favour of a professional force. But the impact of these large military establishments on their home states struck the English as appalling. The greatly increased cost to a country that maintained such an army, and the enhanced power the fighting force gave the ruler, frequently led to a fatal loss of its parliament's political authority. . . .

Unless there was war or the immediate danger of it, Parliament was unwilling to vote the necessary funds for a force of any substantial size. As an island nation, the English could cling to principle with less risk and deny their king this dangerous tool. The Crown had little option but to maintain the militia as an effective fighting force.

Target Practice Mandatory

The English subject's duty to defend himself and his country may have been a source of power and cause for civic boasting—indeed, pamphleteers during the sixteenth, seventeenth, and eighteenth centuries grew increasingly exuberant in their praise of the militia concept—but it was more likely to be regarded as a nuisance by the man called upon to participate. Not only was he put to the expense of obtaining and maintaining the weapons the law required, but he might have to devote several days, possibly longer, to musters [military roll call] and military duty. Just as irksome were the mandatory practice sessions, for the king insisted that the people be expert in the use of the arms they were obliged to possess. Villages were instructed to maintain targets or butts at which local men were to practice, first with the longbow, later with the musket. It is obvious from the number of statutes and proclamations which reiterated these orders that both maintenance of targets and practice sessions were often neglected. An act of Henry VIII, for instance, specified "that butts be made . . . in every city, town, and place, According To The Law of Ancient Time Used, and that the said inhabitants, and dwellers in every of them, be Compelled To Make and Continue Such Butts, upon pain to forfeit, for every three months so lacking, twenty shillings. And that the Said Inhabitants Shall Exercise Themselves With Long-Bows In Shooting At The Same, and elsewhere, in holy days and other times convenient." By the time this was enacted, firearms had begun to replace the longbow. The same act, therefore, permitted lords, knights, esquires, gentlemen, and the inhabitants of every city, borough, and market-town "to have and keep in every of their houses any such hand-gun or hand-guns, of the length of one whole yard . . . to the intent to use and shoot the same, at a butt or bank of earth only . . . whereby they and every of them, by the exercise thereof . . . May The better Aid And Assist To The Defence of This Realm, When Need Shall Require." This was an admission on the king's part of the popularity of firearms amongst his subjects and their use in armies on the Continent.

American Gun Culture Is Rooted in History and Political Ideology

Richard Hofstadter

In the following selection historian Richard Hofstadter traces the cultural and political roots of America's gun culture. He acknowledges that the frontier experience played a role in forging the myth of Americans as self-sufficient settlers who needed their firearms both to defend themselves and to hunt food. He puts more emphasis, however, on the political history of gun ownership. The original colonists were suspicious of central authority and standing armies; they believed that defense against both outside aggression and repressive government depended on a well-armed citizenry. This preference for a citizen militia eventually found its way into the Constitution in the form of the Second Amendment's guarantee of the right to bear arms.

Richard Hofstadter is considered one of the most important American historians of the twentieth century. His work focused on the political and cultural history of the United States as exemplified in his classic work The Paranoid Style in American Politics.

Senator Joseph Tydings of Maryland, appealing in the summer of 1968 for an effective gun-control law, lamented: "It is just tragic that in all of Western civilization the United States is the one country with an insane gun policy." In one respect this was an understatement Western or otherwise, the United States is the only modern industrial urban nation that persists in maintaining a gun culture. It is the only industrial

nation in which the possession of rifles, shotguns, and handguns is lawfully prevalent among large numbers of its population. It is the only such nation that has been impelled in recent years to agonize at length about its own disposition
toward violence and to set up a commission to examine it, the
only nation so attached to the supposed "right" to bear arms
that its laws abet assassins, professional criminals, berserk
murderers, and political terrorists at the expense of the or-
derly population—and, yet it remains, and is apparently determined to remain, the most passive of all major countries in
the matter of gun control. Many otherwise intelligent Americans cling with pathetic stubbornness to the notion that the
people's right to bear arms is the greatest protection of their
individual rights and a firm safeguard of democracy—without
being in the slightest perturbed by the fact that no other democracy in the world observes any such "right" and that in
some democracies in which citizen' rights are rather better
protected than in ours, such as England and the Scandinavian
countries, our arms control policies would be considered
laughable. . . .

It is very easy, in interpreting American history, to give the
credit and the blame for almost everything to the frontier, and
certainly this temptation is particularly strong where guns are
concerned. After all, for the first 250 years of their history
Americans were an agricultural people with a continuing history of frontier expansion. At the very beginning the wild
continent abounded with edible game, and a colonizing people
still struggling to control the wilderness and still living very
close to the subsistence level found wild game an important
supplement to their diet. Moreover, there were no enforceable
feudal inhibitions against poaching by the common man, who
was free to roam where he could and shoot what he could
and who ate better when he shot better. Furthermore, all
farmers, but especially farmers in a lightly settled agricultural

country, need guns for the control of wild vermin and predators. The wolf, as we still say, has to be kept from the door.

Guns Used to Battle Indians

Finally, and no less imperatively, there were the Indians, who were all too often regarded by American frontiersmen as another breed of wild animal. The situation of the Indians, constantly under new pressures from white encroachments, naturally commands modern sympathy. But they were in fact, partly from the very desperation of their case, often formidable, especially in the early days when they were an important force in the international rivalries of England, France, and Spain in North America. Like the white man they had guns, and like him they committed massacres. Modern critics of our culture who, like Susan Sontag, seem to know nothing of American history, who regard the white race as a "cancer" and assert that the United States was "founded on a genocide," may fantasize that the Indians fought according to the rules of the Geneva Convention. But in the tragic conflict of which they were to be the chief victims, they were capable of striking terrible blows. In King Philip's War (1675–76) they damaged half the towns of New England, destroyed a dozen, and killed an estimated one out of sixteen males of military age among the settlers. Later the Deerfield and other frontier massacres left powerful scars on the frontier memory, and in the formative days of the colonial period wariness of sudden Indian raids and semimilitary preparations to combat them were common on the western border of settlements. Men and women, young and old, were all safer if they could command a rifle. "A well grown boy," remembered the Reverend Joseph Doddridge of his years on the Virginia frontier, "at the age of twelve or thirteen years, was furnished with a small rifle and shot-pouch. He then became a fort soldier, and had his porthole assigned him. Hunting squirrels, turkeys, and raccoon, soon made him expert in the use of his gun."

That familiarity with the rifle, which was so generally inculcated on the frontier, had a good deal to do with such successes as Americans had in the battles of the Revolution. The Pennsylvania rifle, developed by German immigrants, was far superior to Brown Bess, the regulation military musket used by British troops. This blunt musket, an inaccurate weapon at any considerable distance, was used chiefly to gain the effect of mass firepower in open field maneuvers at relatively close range. The long, slender Pennsylvania rifle, which had a bored barrel that gave the bullet a spin, had a flatter and more direct trajectory, and in skilled hands it became a precision instrument. More quickly loaded and effective at a considerable distance, it was singularly well adapted not only to the shooting of squirrels but to the woodsman's shoot-and-hide warfare. It struck such terror into the hearts of British regulars as to cause George Washington to ask that as many of his troops as possible be dressed in the frontiersman's hunting shirt, since the British thought "every such person a complete Marksman." The rifle went a long way to make up for the military inconsistencies and indifferent discipline of American militiamen, and its successes helped to instill in the American mind a conviction of the complete superiority of the armed yeoman to the military professionals of Europe.

Guns Used for Sport and Entertainment

What began as a necessity of agriculture and the frontier took hold as a sport and as an ingredient in the American imagination. Before the days of spectator sports, when competitive athletics became a basic part of popular culture, hunting and fishing probably were the chief American sports, sometimes wantonly pursued, as in the decimation of the bison. But for millions of American boys, learning to shoot and above all graduating from toy guns and receiving the first real rifle of their own were milestones of life, veritable rites of passage that certified their arrival at manhood. (It is still argued by some defenders of our gun culture, and indeed conceded by some of its critics, that the gun cannot and will not be given up because it is a basic symbol of masculinity. But the trouble with all such glib Freudian generalities is that they do not explain cultural variations: they do not tell us why men elsewhere have *not* found the gun essential to their masculinity.)

What was so decisive in the winning of the West and the conquest of the Indian became a standard ingredient in popular entertainment. In the penny-dreadful Western and then in films and on television, the western man, quick on the draw, was soon an acceptable hero of violence. He found his successors in the private eye, the FBI agent, and in the gangster himself, who so often provides a semilegitimate object of hero worship, a man with loyalties, courage, and a code of his own—even in films purporting to show that crime does not pay. All mass cultures have their stereotyped heroes, and none are quite free of violence; but the United States has shown an unusual penchant for the isolated, wholly individualistic detective, sheriff, or villain, and its entertainment portrays the solution of melodramatic conflicts much more commonly than, say, the English, as arising not out of ratiocination or some scheme of moral order but out of ready and ingenious violence. Every Walter Mitty has had his moment when he is Gary Cooper, stalking the streets in *High Noon* with his gun at the ready.[1] [The English novelist] D. H. Lawrence may have had something, after all, when he made his characteristically bold, impressionistic, and unflattering judgment that "the essential American soul is hard, isolate, stoic, and a killer." It was the notion cherished also by [American author Ernest] Hemingway in his long romance with war and hunting and with the other sports that end in death.

However, when the frontier and its ramifications are given their due, they fall far short of explaining the persistence of

1. Watter Mitty is a fictional character, an ordinary office worker who fantasizes about being a hero. Gary Cooper was an actor who starred in the 1950s Western classic *High Noon*.

the American gun culture. Why is the gun still so prevalent in a culture in which only about 4 percent of the country's workers now make their living from farming, a culture that for the last century and a half has had only a tiny fragment of its population actually in contact with a frontier, that, in fact, has not known a true frontier for three generations? Why did the United States alone among industrial societies cling to the idea that a substantially unregulated supply of guns among its city populations is a safe and acceptable thing? This is, after all, not the only nation with a frontier history. Canada and Australia have had theirs, and yet their gun control measures are far more satisfactory than ours. Again, Japan, with no frontier but with an ancient tradition of feudal and military violence, has adopted, along with its modernization, such rigorous gun laws that its gun homicide rate ... is one of the world's lowest. (The land of hara-kiri [ritual suicide] also has one of the lowest gun suicide rates—about one-fiftieth of ours.) In sum, other societies, in the course of industrial and urban development, have succeeded in modifying their old gun habits, and we have not.

The Political Appeal of an Armed Citizenry

One factor that could not be left out of any adequate explanation of the tenacity of our gun culture is the existence of an early American political creed that has had a surprisingly long life, albeit much of it now is in an underground popular form. It has to do with the anti-militaristic traditions of radical English Whiggery, which were taken over and intensified in colonial America, especially during the generation preceding the American Revolution, and which became an integral part of the American political tradition. The popular possession of the gun was a central point in a political doctrine that became all but sacrosanct in the Revolution: a doctrine that rested upon faith in the civic virtue and military prowess of the yeoman; belief in the degeneration of England and in the sharp decline of "the liberties of Englishmen" on their original home soil; and a great fear of a standing army as one of the key dangers to this body of ancient liberties. The American answer to civic and military decadence, real or imagined, was the armed yeoman.

By the same reasoning the answer to militarism and standing armies was the militia system. It had long been the contention of those radical Whig writers whose works did so much to set the background of American thought, that liberty and standing armies were incompatible. [Julius] Caesar and [Oliver] Cromwell were commonly cited as the prime historical examples of the destructive effects of political generals on the liberties of the people. The Americans became confident that their alternative device, an armed people, was the only possible solution to the perennial conflict between militarism and freedom. Their concern over the evils of repeated wars and institutionalized armies was heightened by the eighteenth-century European wars in which they were inevitably involved. Blaming the decay that they imagined to be sweeping over England in good part on the increasing role of the military in the mother country, they found their worst fears confirmed by the quartering of troops before the Revolution. John Adams saw in the Boston Massacre "the strongest proof of the danger of standing armies." The Virginian George Mason, surveying the history of the nations of the world, remarked: "What havoc, desolation and destruction, have been perpetrated by standing armies!" The only remedy, he thought, reverting to one of the genial fictions of this school of thought, was the ancient Saxon militia, "the natural strength and only stable security of a free government." [Thomas] Jefferson reverted to the idea of a popular Saxon militia by providing in his first draft of the Virginia Constitution of 1776 that "no freeman shall ever be debarred the use of arms."

The Militia Myth

Washington, who had to command militiamen, had no illusions about them. He had seen not a single instance, he once wrote, that would justify "an opinion of Militia or raw Troops being fit for the real business of fighting. I have found them useful as light Parties to skirmish in the woods, but incapable of making or sustaining a serious attack." Despite the poor record of militia troops in the Revolution, as compared with the courage and persistence of Washington's small and fluctuating Continental Army, the myth persisted that the freedom of America had been won by the armed yeoman and the militia system, and the old fear of a standing army was in no way diminished now that it was not to be under the command of an English aristocracy but of native American generals. In the mid-1780s, when the Americans had won their independence and were living under the Articles of Confederation, Secretary of War Henry Knox found himself the administrator of an army of about seven hundred men. In the 1790s, when it was proposed under the Constitution to add only about five hundred more, Pennsylvania Democrat Senator William Maclay anxiously observed that the government seemed to be "laying the foundation of a standing army"! Only the disastrous performance of militiamen in the War of 1812 persuaded many American leaders that the militia was a slender reed upon which to rest the security of the nation.

In the meantime the passion for a popular militia as against a professional army had found its permanent embodiment in the Second Amendment to the Constitution: "A well regulated Militia, being necessary to the security of a free State, the right of the people to keep and bear Arms, shall not be infringed." By its inclusion in the Bill of Rights, the right to bear arms thus gained permanent sanction in the nation, but it came to be regarded as an item on the basic list of guarantees of *individual* liberties. Plainly it was not meant as such. The right to bear arms was a *collective*, not an individual right, closely linked to the civic need (especially keen in the absence of a sufficient national army) for "a well regulated Militia." It was, in effect, a promise that Congress would not be able to bar the states from doing whatever was necessary to maintain well-regulated militias.

The Militia Act of 1792

United States Congress

At the time of the United States' founding, many politicians had a great fear of standing armies. They worried that the army would become an instrument for a tyrannical government. For defense against internal and external enemies, the framers of the Constitution proposed a militia. Composed of all white male citizens between eighteen and forty-five years of age, the militia was thought to be a safer alternative to a permanent army.

In order for the militia to be effective, however, Congress felt the need to establish uniform rules for its training and governance. It did this with the Militia Act of 1792, excerpted here. The act set out strict rules for the citizens who participated in mandatory militia activities. It required that all militia members provide their own weapons and ammunition, attend training, have their weapons inspected, and be organized into companies and brigades, each with a number of specialized units such as artillery or mounted dragoons.

I. *Be it enacted by the Senate and House of Representatives of the United States of America,* in Congress assembled, That each and every free able-bodied white male citizen of the respective States, resident therein, who is or shall be of [the] age of eighteen years, and under the age of forty-five years (except as is herein after excepted) shall severally and respectively be enrolled in the militia, by the Captain or Commanding Officer of the company, within whose bounds such citizen shall reside, and that within twelve months after the passing of this Act. And it shall at all time hereafter be the duty of every such Captain or Commanding Officer of a company, to enroll every such citizen as aforesaid, and also those who shall, from time to time, arrive at the age of 18 years, or being at the age of 18

United States Congress, "Militia Act of 1792," May 8, 1792.

years, and under the age of 45 years (except as before excepted) shall come to reside within his bounds; and shall without delay notify such citizen of the said enrollment, by the proper non-commissioned Officer of the company, by whom such notice may be proved. That every citizen, so enrolled and notified, shall, within six months thereafter, provide himself with a good musket or firelock, a sufficient bayonet and belt, two spare flints, and a knapsack, a pouch, with a box therein, to contain not less than twenty four cartridges, suited to the bore of his musket or firelock, each cartridge to contain a proper quantity of pow[d]er and ball; or with a good rifle, knapsack, shot-pouch, and pow[d]er-horn, twenty balls suited to the bore of his rifle, and a quarter of a pow[d]er of pow[d]er; and shall appear so armed, accoutred and provided, when called out to exercise or into service, except, that when called out on company days to exercise only, he may appear without a knapsack. That the commissioned Officers shall severally be armed with a sword or *hanger* [short sword], *and espontoon* [pike]; and that from and after five years from the passing of this Act, all muskets from arming the militia as is herein required, shall be of bores sufficient for balls of the eighteenth part of a pound; and every citizen so enrolled, and providing himself with the arms, ammunition and accoutrements, required as aforesaid, shall hold the same exempted from all suits, distresses, executions or sales, for debt or for the payment of taxes.

Exemptions from Militia Duty

II. And be it further enacted, That the Vice-President of the United States, the Officers, judicial and executives, of the government of the United States; the members of both houses of Congress, and their respective officers; all custom house officers, with the clerks; all post officers, and stage-drivers who are employed in the care and conveyance of the mail of the post office of the United States; all Ferrymen employed at any ferry on the post road; all inspectors of exports; all pilots, all mariners actually employed in the sea service of any citizen or merchant within the United States; and all persons who now are or may be hereafter exempted by the laws of the respective states, shall be and are hereby exempted from militia duty, notwithstanding their being above the age of eighteen and under the age of forty-five years.

III. And be it further enacted, That within one year after the passing of the Act, the militia of the respective states shall be arranged into divisions, brigades, regiments, battalions, and companies, as the legislature of each state shall direct; and each division, brigade, and regiment, shall be numbered at the formation thereof; and a record made of such numbers of the Adjutant-General's office in the state; and when in the field, or in serviced in the state, such division, brigade, and regiment shall, respectively, take rank according to their numbers, reckoning the first and lowest number highest in rank. That if the same be convenient, each brigade shall consist of four regiments; each regiment of two battalions; each battalion of five companies; each company of sixty-four privates. That the said militia shall be officered by the respective states, as follows: To each division one Major-General, with two Aids-de-camp, with the rank of major; to each brigade, one brigadier-major, with the rank of a major; to each company, one captain, one lieutenant, one ensign, four serjeants, four corporals, one drummer, and one fifer and bugler. That there shall be a regimental staff, to consist of one adjutant, and one quartermaster, to rank as lieutenants; one paymaster; one surgeon, and one surgeon's mate; one serjeant-major; one drum-major, and one fife-major.

Special Equipment Required

IV. And be it further enacted, That out of the militia enrolled as is herein directed, there shall be formed for each battalion, as least one company of grenadiers, light infantry or riflemen;

and that each division there shall be, at least, one company of
artillery, and one troop of horse: There shall be to each company of artillery, one captain, two lieutenants, four serjeants,
four corporals, six gunners, six bombardiers, one drummer,
and one fifer. The officers to be armed with a sword or hanger,
a fusee, bayonet and belt, with a cartridge box to contain
twelve cartridges; and each private of [the artillary crew] shall
furnish themselves with good horses of at least fourteen hands
and an half high, and to be armed with a sword and pair of
pistols, the holsters of which to be covered with bearskin caps.
Each dragoon [mounted soldier] to furnish himself with a
serviceable horse, at least fourteen hands and an half high, a
good saddle, bridle, mail-pillion and valise, holster, and a best
plate and crupper [strap] matross, a pair of boots and spurs; a
pair of pistols, a sabre, and a cartouchbox to contain twelve
cartridges for pistols. That each company of artillery and
troop of horse shall be formed of volunteers from the brigade,
at the discretion of the Commander in Chief of the State, not
exceeding one company of each to a regiment, nor more in
number than one eleventh part of the infantry, and shall be
uniformly clothed in raiments, to be furnished at their expense, the colour and fashion to be determined by the Briga-
dier commanding the brigade to which they belong.

V. *And be it further enacted*, That each battalion and regiment shall be provided with the state and regimental colours
by the Field-Officers, and each company with a drum and fife
or bugle-horn, by the commissioned officers of the company,
in such manner as the legislature of the respective States shall
direct. . . .

Regular Inspections

X. *And be it further enacted*, That it shall be the duty of the
brigade inspector, to attend the regimental and battalion meeting of the militia composing their several brigades, during the
time of their being under arms, to inspect their arms, ammu-

nition and accoutrements; superintend their exercise and maneuvres and introduce the system of military discipline before described, throughout the brigade, agreeable to law, and such orders as they shall from time to time receive from the commander in Chief of the State; to make returns to the adjutant general of the state at least once in every year, of the militia of the brigade to which he belongs, reporting therein the actual situation of the arms, accoutrement, and ammunition, of the several corps, and every other thing which, in his judgment, may relate to their government and general advancement of good order and military discipl[in]e; an adjutant general shall make a return of all militia of the state, to the Commander in Chief of the said state, and a duplicate of the same to the president of the United States.

Rampant Violence Prompts Early Attempts at Gun Control

William Weir

In the following selection William Weir describes the passage of the first gun control laws in the United States, which originated in the frontier states. Legislatures of these states, starting with Kentucky in 1813, sought to curb the mounting violence in their new settlements. With frontiersmen carrying hidden knives and pistols, many quarrels—from arguments over competing land claims to accusations of cheating at cards—escalated into deadly confrontations. The Kentucky legislature therefore decided to outlaw the carrying of concealed weapons. There were no arguments about the new laws' violation of the Constitution's Second Amendment because at the time the Bill of Rights was thought to apply only to the federal government. Each state, and sometimes even each municipality, was left to legislate its own gun laws.

William Weir is a journalist who is a member of both Handgun Control, Inc. and the National Rifle Association, although he opposes most of the actions of both organizations.

The War of 1812 was still raging when Kentucky passed the first weapons control law. It was certainly not intended to disarm the militia. The Kentucky militia, in particular, was extremely active during the war. It participated in the attempts to invade Canada and again proved what every militia but the Swiss have repeatedly demonstrated: militia are useless for anything but defending their homes. At the end of the war (actually after the peace treaty had been signed), Kentucky's

William Weir, *A Well Regulated Militia: The Battle over Gun Control*. North Haven, CT: Archon Books, 1997, pp. 35–37. © 1997 William Weir. All rights reserved. Reproduced by permission of the author.

citizen-soldiers also participated in the most resounding victory any militia ever scored against regular troops—the Battle of New Orleans.

Concealed Weapons Targeted

The lawmakers of Kentucky had no problem with citizens carrying muskets or, more usually, rifles. They worried about concealed weapons. In 1813, when they passed their pioneering weapons control law, Kentucky was a frontier state. And the "wild West" of the early nineteenth century was far wilder than the California goldfields and the Great Plains became in mid and late century. There were no effective police, and few courtrooms and jails. There were plenty of disputes, though. Land claims, card games, and just plain cussedness led to fights. The nature of the frontier was such that it attracted the most aggressive and ruthless of the citizens of the eastern seaboard. Also, most of the new Westerners had been Southerners, and Southerners had somehow arrived at the conclusion that they were all aristocrats and that hypersensitivity to slights was aristocratic behavior. Men carried sword canes, hid daggers under their coattails, and kept small pistols in their pockets. And they were not slow to use them.

The Kentucky law was aimed at concealed weapons. No one saw any conflict with the Second Amendment. As a matter of fact, most of the few people who considered the question at all believed amendments to the U.S. Constitution did not apply to state laws. (And the U.S. Supreme Court, in *Barron v. Baltimore*, later in the first half of the century ruled that it did not.) That was a moot point, because most state constitutions also protected the right of the people to keep and bear arms. Those that didn't, like Connecticut's, provided for the calling up of a militia composed of all males of military age, all of whom were expected to have their own weapons. The Kentucky legislators, though, did not consider "dirk knives," pocket pistols, and sword canes to be particularly useful militia weapons. They based their decision on a developing legal doctrine called "the police power of the state." The doctrine appears to be based on the Tenth Amendment to the U.S. Constitution: "The powers not delegated to the United States by the Constitution, nor prohibited by it to the States, are reserved to the States respectively, or to the people" —on that, and on a desire to curb an epidemic of personal violence. Louisiana passed a similar law at the same time.

The neighboring frontier state of Indiana thought Kentucky's idea was a good one and adopted a similar law in 1819. The laws, unfortunately, did not curb violence. Violence spread, and the tools of violence continued to be developed.

In 1822, the Kentucky Court of Appeals, the state's highest court, voided the 1813 law. It found the law in conflict with the Kentucky Constitution, which stated "that the right of the citizens to bear arms in defense of themselves and the state shall not be questioned." The Louisiana high court upheld the law because it did not affect the right of a citizen to carry weapons but only concealed weapons.

Weapons and Weapons Laws Spread

Around 1830, Henry Deringer of Philadelphia developed his famous pocket pistol. It sold in tremendous numbers in the West. In a few years it was carried by men in all parts of the country and from all walks of life. Senators and stevedores, gamblers and grocers all carried one of Deringer's products or one of the host of imitations it inspired. About the same time the Deringer pocket pistol was born, James Bowie acquired the huge single-edge knife that bears his name. Bowie's use of the knife made him nationally famous. The Bowie knife spread as fast as the derringer (uncapitalized and with a change of spelling that quickly became the generic name for all small, large-bore pistols). The Bowie knife settled barroom brawls and formal duels. It was named as the weapon to be used in at least one duel between two congressmen. From Washington to San Francisco, the Bowie knife and the derringer became standard equipment for quarrelsome and tetchy men. The highest per capita possession of both weapons, though, was in the Old Southwest. That area, too, was the home of the "push dagger," a distinctively American weapon with a handle set at right angles to the blade for easier concealment. The push dagger, hung upside down under the armpit in a sheath with a spring retainer, was many a gambler's best friend. The southwestern frontier states of Arkansas and Georgia passed concealed weapons laws in 1837. However, the Georgia law, which banned the private *possession* of pistols, was declared unconstitutional because, according to the Georgia Supreme Court,

> The right of the whole people, old and young, men, women and boys, and not the militia only, to keep and bear arms of every description, and not such merely as are used by the militia, shall not be infringed . . . in the slightest degree; and all this for the important end to be obtained, the rearing up and qualifying of a well-regulated militia, so vitally necessary to a free state.

In 1838, Virginia, which included what is now West Virginia, passed a weapons law. By 1850, every western state had passed laws barring the carrying of concealed weapons. After the Civil War, the states of the far West, where most settlements were small and had many miles of empty space between them, often left weapons regulation up to local authorities. That led to banning weapons within the city limits and having travelers check their weapons on entering a town and taking them back as they were leaving. Sometimes the travelers checked their weapons. More often, both strangers and residents carried revolvers hidden in their pockets. Photos of such rip-roaring cow towns as Dodge City [Kansas] taken in the 1870s and 1880s show no holsters and cartridge belts being worn. But most of the men were carrying guns.

In the Northeast, at that time, there were no weapons laws. Eastern clothing manufacturers in the period sewed holsters into the right hip pocket of every pair of pants they made. Of course, the customer would be carrying a gun.

Outlawing Private Militias

William Allan Woods

In 1875 a German immigrant named Herman Presser formed an organization devoted to the goal of "improving the mental and bodily condition of its members so as to qualify them for the duties of citizens of a republic." Presser was arrested for violating Articles Five and Six of the Illinois Military Code, which held that no armed formations could be organized without the approval of the governor. Presser fought his case all the way to the Supreme Court. He argued that the Illinois law violated his right to "keep and bear arms" found in the Second Amendment and his right to due process found in the Fourteenth Amendment.

The Supreme Court decided against Presser. Writing for the majority, Justice William Allan Woods held that the Second Amendment merely prohibited the federal Congress from passing laws to limit the right to bear arms; it did not forbid states from regulating armed militias—especially those that were not government-sanctioned.

William Allan Woods was appointed to the Supreme Court in 1880 after a long career as a lawyer and judge. He served on the Court until his death in 1887.

W e ... inquire whether the fifth and sixth sections of article 11 of the Military Code are in violation of ... provisions of the constitution of the United States relied on by the plaintiff [Presser] in error. The first of these is the second amendment, which declares: 'A well regulated militia being necessary to the security of a free state, the right of the people to keep and bear arms shall not be infringed.'

William Allan Woods, *Presser v. State of Illinois*, U.S. Supreme Court, 1886.

Second Amendment Limits Congress

We think it clear that the sections under consideration, which only forbid bodies of men to associate together as military organizations, or to drill or parade with arms in cities and towns unless authorized by law, do not infringe the right of the people to keep and bear arms. But a conclusive answer to the contention that this amendment prohibits the legislation in question lies in the fact that the amendment is a limitation only upon the power of congress and the national government, and not upon that of the state. It was so held by this court in the case of *U.S. v. Cruikshank*, in which the chief justice, in delivering the judgment of the court, said that the right of the people to keep and bear arms 'is not a right granted by the constitution.' Neither is it in any manner dependent upon that instrument for its existence. The second amendment declares that it shall not be infringed, but this, as has been seen, means no more than that it shall not be infringed by congress. This is one of the amendments that has no other effect than to restrict the powers of the national government, leaving the people to look for their protection against any violation by their fellow-citizens of the rights it recognizes to what is called in *City of New York v. Miln*, the 'powers which relate to merely municipal legislation, or what was perhaps more properly called internal police,' 'not surrendered or restrained' by the constitution of the United States.'

It is undoubtedly true that all citizens capable of bearing arms constitute the reserved military force or reserve militia of the United States as well as of the states, and, in view of this prerogative of the general government, as well as of its general powers, the states cannot, even laying the constitutional provision in question out of view, prohibit the people from keeping and bearing arms, so as to deprive the United States of their rightful resource for maintaining the public security, and disable the people from performing their duty to the general government. But, as already stated, we think it clear that the sections under consideration do not have this effect.

No Right to Drill in Military Formation

The plaintiff in error next insists that the sections of the Military Code of Illinois under which he was indicted are an invasion of that clause of the first section of the fourteenth amendment to the constitution of the United States which declares: 'No state shall make or enforce any law which shall abridge the privileges or immunities of citizens of the United States.' It is only the privileges and immunities of citizens of the United States that the clause relied on was intended to protect. A state may pass laws to regulate the privileges and immunities of its own citizens, provided that in so doing it does not abridge their privileges and immunities as citizens of the United States. The inquiry is therefore pertinent, what privilege or immunity of a citizen of the United States is abridged by sections 5 and 6 of article 11 of the Military Code of Illinois? The plaintiff in error was not a member of the organized volunteer militia of the state of Illinois, nor did he belong to the troops of the United States or to any organization under the militia law of the United States. On the contrary, the fact that he did not belong to the organized militia or the troops of the United States was an ingredient in the offense for which he was convicted and sentenced. The question is, therefore, had he a right as a citizen of the United States, in disobedience of the state law, to associate with others as a military company, and to drill and parade with arms in the towns and cities of the state? If the plaintiff in error has any such privilege, he must be able to point to the provision of the constitution or statutes of the United States by which it is conferred. For, as was said by this court in *U.S. v. Cruikshank*, the government of the

United States, although it is 'within the scope of its powers supreme and above the states,' 'can neither grant nor secure to its citizens any right or privilege not expressly or by implication placed under its jurisdiction.' 'All that cannot be so granted or so secured are left to the exclusive protection of the state.' We have not been referred to any statute of the United States which confers upon the plaintiff in error the privilege which he asserts. The only clause in the constitution which, upon any pretense, could be said to have any relation whatever to his right to associate with others as a military company, is found in the first amendment, which declares that 'congress shall make no laws . . . abridging . . . the right of the people peaceably to assemble and to petition the government for a redress of grievances.' This is a right, which it was held in *U.S. v. Cruikshank*, above cited, was an attribute of national citizenship, and, as such, under the protection of, and guarantied by, the United States. But it was held in the same case that the right peaceably to assemble was not protected by the clause referred to, unless the purpose of the assembly was to petition the government for a redress of grievances. The right voluntarily to associate together as a military company or organization, or to drill or parade with arms, without, and independent of, an act of congress or law of the state authorizing the same, is not an attribute of national citizenship. Military organization and military drill and parade under arms are subjects especially under the control of the government of every country. They cannot be claimed as a right independent of law. Under our political system they are subject to the regulation and control of the state and federal governments, acting in due regard to their respective prerogatives and powers. The constitution and laws of the United States will be searched in vain for any support to the view that these rights are privileges and immunities of citizens of the United States independent of some specific legislation on the subject.

State Governments Can
Regulate Associations

It cannot be successfully questioned that the state governments, unless restrained by their own constitutions, have the power to regulate or prohibit associations and meetings of the people, except in the case of peaceable assemblies to perform the duties or exercise the privileges of citizens of the United States, and have also the power to control and regulate the organization, drilling, and parading of military bodies and associations, except when such bodies or associations are authorized by the militia laws of the United States. The exercise of this power by the states is necessary to the public peace, safety, and good order. To deny the power would be to deny the right of the state to disperse assemblages organized for sedition and treason, and the right to suppress armed mobs bent on riot and rapine.

CHAPTER 2

Debating the Purpose of the Second Amendment

Chapter Preface

The Second Amendment reads, "A well regulated Militia, being necessary to the security of a free State, the right of the people to keep and bear Arms, shall not be infringed." Proponents and opponents of gun control interpret this text in radically different ways. Proponents of gun control point to the first clause, claiming it shows that the amendment applies only to state-organized militias. At the time of ratification of the Constitution, the militia generally consisted of all male citizens of military age, around eighteen to forty-five years old. The militiamen were required to supply their own weapons. Therefore, gun control proponents say, the Second Amendment was intended simply to ensure that militias could be well armed, not to protect an individual right to bear arms separate from the context of militias.

Supporters of gun rights also look at the context of militias, but come to an opposite conclusion. They point out that militia membership implied both duties and rights. One of those rights was the individual right to defend one's home and family. Gun rights advocates look to early commentaries on firearms ownership, both in England and the United States, to support their belief that gun ownership is an individual right.

In legal terms, it seems that gun control advocates have the upper hand. In *Miller v. United States* (1934), the U.S. Supreme Court held that the Second Amendment did link the right to possess firearms to a "well regulated Militia." The ruling said that possession of a sawed-off shotgun could not be justified by any legitimate militia-related purpose; therefore, the government could outlaw such weapons.

Gun rights advocates respond that current scholarship has cast doubt on the *Miller* decision. The concept of an "armed people" was important to the framers of the Constitution and the English liberal philosophers who influenced them. This "armed people" is the final guarantee of the citizenry's liberty against tyrannical government. The framers built the right to "keep and bear arms" into the Constitution to ensure that future governments could not eliminate the ultimate check on their power.

No doubt controversy over the meaning of the Second Amendment will continue. The Supreme Court's decision in *Miller* did not stop the debate; any future ruling by the Court on gun rights will probably be just as disputed.

The Second Amendment as Viewed by Gun Rights Supporters

Constance Emerson Crooker

Constance Emerson Crooker is a writer and retired attorney. In the following excerpt she summarizes the arguments made by gun rights advocates regarding the meaning of the Second Amendment. They hold that the Second Amendment protects the right of individuals to bear arms, not the right of states to organize militias, as some gun control proponents claim. They base this conclusion on the U.S. Constitution, which contains clauses concerning the regulation of state militias; the Second Amendment would have been redundant, they argue, if its purpose was to assure the various states the right to organize these groups. Instead, they insist that the amendment protects the individual's right to be armed. In addition, gun rights advocates look to statements by Revolutionary-era leaders who insisted that the right of the people to bear arms was the ultimate defense against tyranny.

Gun rights advocates and gun control proponents divide most sharply in their view of who or what receives Second Amendment protection. Gun rights advocates assert that the Second Amendment was designed to protect individuals in their private capacities. Their best arguments follow.

The Second Amendment Guarantees Individual Rights

The Second Amendment extends a right to individuals to possess and use firearms in the defense of themselves and their homes. [In the words of legal scholar Leonard Levy,] "Believing that the amendment does not authorize an individual's right." Nineteenth-century constitutional commentators [in the words of a National Rifle Association (NRA) legal brief,] "took it for granted that the Second Amendment protects the right of individuals to keep and bear arms."

The intent of the framers of the Constitution was that every man retain the right to be armed. James Madison spoke of European governments that were "afraid to trust the people with arms," and he spoke of "the advantage of being armed, which the Americans possess over the people of almost every other nation." [The Revolutionary War leader] Patrick Henry, who opposed ratification of the Constitution partly out of fear the federal government would seize control over weapons and their use, said, "The great object is that every man be armed. . . . Everyone who is able may have a gun."

If the Second Amendment means that the states are assured of the right to maintain their own militias, why would the Founders have rejected a Virginia/North Carolina proposal that each state shall have the power to organize, arm, and discipline its own militia when Congress fails to do so? That rejected provision cannot embody the true meaning of the Second Amendment.

Looking to history, each side agrees that, at the time of the American Revolution, there existed a widespread fear of the capacity for abuse by standing armies. They also agree that the militia was composed of citizenry subject to occasional military duty, and that the men called up were to appear with their own firearms and other equipment. But gun rights advocates point out that the militia was viewed as the opposite of a formal military organization. It was a stand-by force made up of armed citizens, who constituted a broad segment of the population. Because standing armies were feared as a dangerous tool of would-be tyrants, an essentially civilian militia was seen as a safer alternative. It remained inactive until its services were needed, and it remained armed while inactive.

This history still echoes in present law. Gun control proponents are quick to point out how the militia described in Article I, Section 8 of the Constitution evolved into the present-day National Guard. Today's "organized militia" consists of the National Guard and the dwindling Naval Militia. Perhaps, they suggest, the guarantees of the Second Amendment extend only to members of those organizations.

But, say gun rights advocates, they miss the fact that we still have an "unorganized militia" in the United States. Starting with the Militia Act of May 8, 1792, and continuing into the present, as embodied in the U.S. Code, the unorganized militia consists of all able-bodied males between ages seventeen and forty-five, who "are not members of the National Guard or the Naval Militia." In other words, the bulk of our male population is still, under federal law, part of our stand-by militia.

"The People" Means *All* the People

Interestingly, the gun rights advocates do not lean heavily on the existence of this "unorganized militia" as a rationale for the Second Amendment's guarantee. These advocates assert that the Second Amendment's term, "the people" means all the people, and is not limited to a subgroup comprising the organized or unorganized militia. As one pro-rights attorney [federal public defender David Guinn] has said, "The 'people' means the people. What else could it mean?" Even extending the Second Amendment's guarantees to all able-bodied seventeen- to forty-five-year-old males would constitute a restriction on what they view as a universal right.

Gun rights advocates disagree with gun control proponents over the meaning of the phrase "well regulated militia." Control proponents say "well regulated" refers only to an organized militia, such as our present-day National Guard.

Rights advocates [such as the NRA] say that "well regulated" means "not inappropriately regulated" or "not heavily regulated." Because Article I authorizes Congress to standardize the training for the militias, the Second Amendment would not have been created to duplicate such training and regulation. They conclude that the Amendment must be a prohibition against civilian disarmament.

For historical support, they point out that the "shot heard 'round the world" at the start of the Revolutionary War was fired when the British governor sent troops to collect and destroy colonists' firearms in Lexington and Concord, Massachusetts. The governor believed the colonists were too heavily armed. In Lexington, the British Force was confronted by "people drawn up in military order." Then, after the British seized firearms in Concord, Concord residents ambushed, shot, and killed the British on their return march to Boston. So the American Revolution began with citizens' resistance when the government attempted to disarm them. A gun rights advocate [namely, the Citizens Committee for the Right to Keep And Bear Arms] has asserted, "The historical evidence is unquestionable that the Second Amendment was prompted in part by the British policy of confiscating the firearms of individuals."

But this argument brings us full circle. If the armed colonists of Lexington and Concord were acting as members of their militia, it is just as reasonable to argue that the Founders were concerned about the government seizing weapons from individuals acting in the capacity of militiamen.

No States' Rights Purpose to Second Amendment

According to gun rights advocates, the Second Amendment was not about granting the states power over their militias. When the Constitution granted almost complete federal authority over state militias, the Anti-Federalists were quick to denounce the power shift from the states to the federal government. In 1787, Attorney General Luther Martin commented on Article I, Section 8 of the Constitution, which gave the federal government broad powers to supervise and call up the state militias. Martin referred to the section as "this extraordinary provision, by which the militia, the only defense and protection which the State can have for the security of their rights against arbitrary encroachments of the general government, is taken entirely out of the power of the respective states, and placed under the power of Congress."

So, when Madison made his famous statement about the advantage of Americans being armed, he was trying to placate the Anti-Federalists with the assurance that, although the federal government had already taken considerable constitutional control over the states' militias, the federal government would, under the Second Amendment, still lack the power to disarm citizens. The "Federalists and the Anti-Federalists *shared* the assumption that the new federal government should lack the power to disarm the citizenry."

In other words, the Second Amendment was not designed to guarantee the states that they could maintain power over their militia. The states had already lost much of that power, and both Federalists and Anti-Federalists were well aware of that. Therefore, the purpose of the Second Amendment was to assure Anti-Federalists that, at least, the people could remain armed.

If it were as the gun control proponents argue, it would be a case of the right hand giving while the left hand takes away. Article I, Section 8, Clause 16 of the Constitution grants Congress the power to take substantial control over state militias. Then, in Article I, Section 10, Clause 3, the states are forbidden to keep troops without the consent of Congress. Then, according to gun control proponents, the Second Amendment, without changing those constitutional provisions, somehow shifts control over militias back to the states. Gun rights advocates assert that, logically, that could not have been the purpose of the Second Amendment. "In fact," says one such advocate, "if one took the purpose attributed to the Second Amendment by the states' rights theorists seriously, it would seem to follow that *all* federal gun control regulations are invalid because control over the private possession of arms lies exclusively in the state governments."

Anti-Tyranny Function of Second Amendment

While gun control proponents argue that the Founders feared insurrection, and would not condone any right of individuals to forcefully oppose an elected government, gun rights advocates claim that a primary purpose of the Second Amendment was to allow individuals enough power to overthrow a tyrannical regime. They find support in the language of English legal theorist Sir William Blackstone (later quoted with approval by Samuel Adams), who, a decade before the American Revolution, said that the right to arms serves "the natural right of resistance and self-preservation, when the sanctions of society and laws are found insufficient to restrain the violence of oppression."

A noted Federalist [Tench Coxe] was quoted in a 1789 newspaper with this comment on the recently proposed Second Amendment: "As civil rulers, not having their duty to the people duly before them, may attempt to tyrannize, and as the military forces which must be occasionally raised to defend our country, might pervert their power to the injury of their fellow-citizens, the people are confirmed by [the Second Amendment] in their right to keep and bear their private arms."

This anti-tyranny rationale for the Amendment was stated by Justice Joseph Story who declared, "The right of the citizens to keep and bear arms has justly been considered, as the palladium of the liberties of the republic; since it offers a strong moral check against usurpation and arbitrary power of the rulers; and will generally, even if these are successful in the first instance, enable the people to resist and triumph over them." Story also wrote, "One of the ordinary modes by which tyrants accomplish their purpose without resistance is, by disarming the people, and making it an offense to keep arms. . . ."

Gun control proponents counter this argument by saying that, even if there were an anti-tyranny function of the Second Amendment, it is now outmoded. Today, few worry that the U.S. Army will impose a military dictatorship over Americans. Nor would bands of armed citizens have much chance of defeating such well-armed forces.

Gun rights advocates respond that an armed populace still creates a deterrent to government oppression by raising the potential costs of military force, even where a military dictatorship would prevail with a sufficient investment of resources.

Anti-Tyranny Function Is Not Obsolete

Furthermore, according to Wayne LaPierre, chief executive officer of the National Rifle Association, the argument that the Second Amendment's anti-tyranny function is obsolete is wrong. "The claim that an armed populace cannot successfully resist assault stems from an unproved theory." He cites examples where guerrilla warfare has triumphed over modern armies, and says, "a determined people who have the means to maintain prolonged war against a modern army can battle it to a standstill, subverting major portions of the army or defeating it themselves or with major arms supplied by outside forces." This leaves one wondering which "outside forces" LaPierre imagines might supply major arms to disgruntled Americans who would band together to throw off the perceived "tyranny" of our federal government.

It should be pointed out that, although the gun rights proponents have amassed strong enough historical arguments to sway one federal circuit court to adopt the personal rights interpretation of the Second Amendment, they may have shot themselves in the foot, so to speak. Their legal briefs on the subject of the Second Amendment reflect a sophisticated view of the historical underpinnings of the Second Amendment, but when gun rights proponents make public declarations regarding Second Amendment rights, they have all the depth of advertising slogans. They tend to portray the founding fathers as unanimously and vigorously defending the right to bear arms, when the reality is that the Second Amendment was forged in order to compromise a hotly debated matter.

The Second Amendment Protects an Individual Right

Sanford Levinson

In an influential law journal article, University of Texas Law School professor Sanford Levinson disputes the claim that the Second Amendment protects only the rights of states to organize militias. According to Levinson, the framers of the Constitution were heavily influenced by liberal English writers of the seventeenth and early eighteenth century. These writers believed that an armed "yeomanry" —a population of small farmers—would be a check against the tyranny of a powerful king. Only such a force, organized into a militia, would be able to defeat a king or other central power in the event that the people's rights were infringed. Thus the militias—composed of all the "peaceable" male citizens—were the last refuge of liberty. By ignoring this concept of an armed people, Levinson argues, constitutional scholars who hold that the Second Amendment guarantees only the right of states to maintain National Guard units are distorting the meaning of the the right to "keep and bear arms."

Recall the Second Amendment: "A well regulated Militia being necessary to the security of a free State, the right of the people to keep and bear Arms shall not be infringed." No one has ever described the Constitution as a marvel of clarity, and the Second Amendment is perhaps one of the worst drafted of all its provisions. What is special about the Amendment is the inclusion of an opening clause—a preamble, if you will—that seems to set out its purpose. No similar clause is part of any other Amendment, though that does not, of course, mean that we do not ascribe purposes to them. It

Sanford Levinson, "The Embarrassing Second Amendment," *Yale Law Journal*, vol. 99, December 1989, pp. 643–49. Copyright © 1989 The Yale Law Journal Company, Inc. Reproduced by permission of the Yale Law Journal Company and William S. Hein Company.

would be impossible to make sense of the Constitution if we did not engage in the ascription [assigning] of purpose. Indeed, the major debates about The First Amendment arise precisely when one tries to discern a purpose, given that "literalism" is a hopelessly failing approach to interpreting it. We usually do not even recognize punishment of fraud—a classic speech act—as a free speech problem because we so sensibly assume that the purpose of the First Amendment could not have been, for example, to protect the circulation of patently deceptive information to potential investors in commercial enterprises. The sharp differences that distinguish those who would limit the reach of the First Amendment to "political" speech from those who would extend it much further, encompassing non-deceptive commercial speech, are all derived from different readings of the purpose that underlies the raw text.

Individual vs. States' Rights

A standard move of those legal analysts who wish to limit the Second Amendment's force is to focus on its "preamble" as setting out a restrictive purpose. Recall [Harvard law professor] Laurence Tribe's assertion that the purpose was to allow the states to keep their militias and to protect them against the possibility that the new national government will use its power to establish a powerful standing army and eliminate the state militias. This purposive reading quickly disposes of any notion that there is an "individual" right to keep and bear arms. The right, if such it be, is only a states's right. The consequence of this reading is obvious: the national government has the power to regulate—to the point of prohibition— private ownership of guns, since that has, by stipulation, nothing to do with preserving state militias. This is, indeed, the position of the ACLU [American Civil Liberties Union], which reads the Amendment as protecting only the right of "maintaining an effective state militia. . . . [T]he individual's right to bear arms applies only to the preservation or efficiency of a well-regulated [state] militia. Except for lawful police and military purposes, the possession of weapons by individuals is not constitutionally protected."

This is not a wholly implausible reading, but one might ask why the Framers did not simply say something like "Congress shall have no power to prohibit state-organized and directed militias." Perhaps they in fact meant to do something else. Moreover, we might ask if ordinary readers of the late 18th century legal prose would have interpreted it as meaning something else. The text at best provides only a starting point for a conversation. In this specific instance, it does not come close to resolving the questions posed by federal regulation of arms. Even if we accept the preamble as significant, we must still try to figure out what might be suggested by guaranteeing to "the people the right to keep and bear arms;" moreover, as we shall see presently, even the preamble presents unexpected difficulties in interpretation.

History of the Second Amendment

One might argue (and some have) that the substantive right is one pertaining to a collective body—"the people"—rather than to individuals. Professor [Lawrence] Cress, for example, argues that state constitutions regularly use the words "man" or "person" in regard to "individual rights such as freedom of conscience," whereas the use in those constitutions of the term "the people" in regard to a right to bear arms is intended to refer to the "sovereign citizenry" collectively organized. Such an argument founders, however, upon examination of the text of the federal Bill of Rights itself and the usage there of the term "the people" in the First, Fourth, Ninth, and Tenth Amendments.

Consider that the Fourth Amendment protects "[t]he right of the people to be secure in their persons," or that the First Amendment refers to the "right of the people peaceably to assemble, and to petition the Government for a redress of grievances." It is difficult to know how one might plausibly read the Fourth Amendment as other than a protection of indi-

65

vidual rights, and it would approach the frivolous to read the assembly and petition clause as referring only to the right of state legislators to meet and pass a remonstrance directed to Congress or the President against some government act. The Tenth Amendment is trickier, though it does explicitly differentiate between "state" and "the people" in terms of retained rights. Concededly, it would be possible to read the Tenth Amendment as suggesting only an ultimate right to revolution by the collective people should the "states" stray too far from their designated role of protecting the rights of the people. This reading follows directly from the social contract theory of the state. (But, of course, many of these rights are held by individuals.)

Although the record is suitably complicated, it seems tendentious to reject out of hand the argument that one purpose of the Amendment was to recognize an individual's right to engage in armed self-defense against criminal conduct. Historian Robert E. Shalhope supports this view, arguing in his article *The Ideological Origins of the Second Amendment* that the Amendment guarantees individuals the right "to possess arms for their own personal defense." It would be especially unsurprising if this were the case, given the fact that the development of a professional police force (even within large American cities) was still at least half a century away at the end of the colonial period. I shall return later in this essay to this individualist notion of the Amendment, particularly in regard to the argument that "changing circumstances," including the development of a professional police force, have deprived it of any continuing plausibility. But I want now to explore a second possible purpose of the Amendment, which as a sometime political theorist I find considerably more interesting.

The Meaning of "Militia"

Assume, as Professor Cress has argued, that the Second Amendment refers to a communitarian, rather than an individual right. We are still left the task of defining the relationship between the community and the state apparatus. It is this fascinating problem to which I now turn.

Consider once more the preamble and its reference to the importance of a well-regulated militia. Is the meaning of the term obvious? Perhaps we should make some effort to find out what the term "militia" meant to 18th century readers and writers.

I, for one, have been persuaded that the term "militia" did not have the limited reference that Professor Cress and many modern legal analysts assign to it. There is strong evidence that "militia" refers to all of the people, or at least all of those treated as full citizens of the community. Consider, for example, the question asked by George Mason, one of the Virginians who refused to sign the Constitution because of its lack of a Bill of Rights: "Who are the Militia? They consist now of the whole people." Similarly, the Federal Farmer, one of the most important Anti-Federalist opponents of the Constitution, referred to a "militia, when properly formed, [as] in fact the people themselves." We have, of course, moved now from text to history. And this history is most interesting, especially when we look at the development of notions of popular sovereignty. It has become almost a cliché of contemporary American historiography to link the development of American political thought, including its constitutional aspects, to republican thought in England, the "country" critique of the powerful "court" centered in London.

The Importance of an Armed Populace

One of the school's important writers, of course, was James Harrington [1611–1677], who not only was influential at the time but also has recently been given a certain pride of place by one of the most prominent of contemporary "neo-republicans," [Harvard history] professor Frank Michelman. One historian describes Harrington as having made "the most significant contribution to English libertarian attitudes toward arms, the individual, and society." He was a central figure in the development of the ideas of popular sovereignty and republicanism. For Harrington, preservation of republican liberty requires independence, which rests primarily on possession of adequate property to make men free from coercion by employers or landlords. But widespread ownership of land is not sufficient. These independent yeomen should also bear arms. As [Yale history] professor [Edmund] Morgan puts it, "[T]hese independent yeomen, armed and embodied in a militia, are also a popular government's best protection against its enemies, whether they be aggressive foreign monarchs or scheming demagogues within the nation itself."

A central fear of Harrington and of all future republicans was a standing army, composed of professional soldiers. Harrington and his fellow republicans viewed a standing army as a threat to freedom, to be avoided at almost all costs. Thus, says Morgan, "A militia is the only safe form of military power that a popular government can employ; and because it is composed of the armed yeomanry, it will prevail over the mercenary professionals who man the armies of neighboring monarchs."

Scholars of the First Amendment have made us aware of the importance of John Trenchard and Thomas Gordon, whose *Cato's Letters* [1720–1723] were central to the formation of the American notion of freedom of the press. That notion includes what [University of Virginia law professor] Vincent Blasi would come to call the "checking value" of a free press, which stands as a sturdy exposer of governmental misdeeds. Consider the possibility, though, that the unlimited "checking value" in a republican polity is the ability of an armed populace, presumptively motivated by a shared commitment to the common good, to resist governmental tyranny. Indeed, one of Cato's letters refers to "the Exercise of despotick Power [as] the unrelenting War of an armed Tyrant upon his unarmed Subjects. . . ."

No Right to Disarm Peaceful Citizens

Cress persuasively shows that no one defended universal possession of arms. New Hampshire had no objection to disarming those who "are or have been in actual rebellion," just as Samuel Adams stressed that only "peaceable citizens" should be protected in their right of "keeping their own arms." All these points can be conceded, however, without conceding as well that Congress—or, for that matter, the States—had the power to disarm these "peaceable citizens."

Surely one of the foundations of American political thought of the period was the well-justified concern about political corruption and consequent governmental tyranny. Even the Federalists, fending off their opponents who accused them of foisting an oppressive new scheme upon the American people, were careful to acknowledge the risks of tyranny. James Madison, for example, speaks in *Federalist* [Paper] Number Forty-Six of "the advantage of being armed, which the Americans possess over the people of almost every other nation." The advantage in question was not merely the defense of American borders; a standing army might well accomplish that. Rather, an armed public was advantageous in protecting political liberty. It is therefore no surprise that the Federal Farmer, the nom de plume of an anti-federalist critic of the new Constitution and its absence of a Bill of Rights, could write that "to preserve liberty, it is essential that the whole body of the people always possess arms, and be taught alike, especially when young, how to use them. . . ." On this matter, at least, there was no cleavage between the pro-ratification Madison and his opponent.

The Second Amendment Does Not Prohibit Gun Regulation

David W. Clark

In the following excerpt from congressional testimony, David W. Clark argues that gun control is both constitutional and necessary for public safety. He insists that gun control has repeatedly been ruled constitutional by the U.S. Supreme Court and lower courts. For over sixty years, starting with United States v. Miller *(1939), the Supreme Court has clearly stated that the phrase "well regulated militia" found in the Second Amendment means that the amendment was intended to protect the right of states to form militias. Moreover, the militias referred to were strictly organized by the state and subject to state law. The right to bear arms, therefore, does not apply to individuals per se, but only to participants in units that are controlled by the various states.*

David W. Clark is an attorney practicing in Jackson, Mississippi, who is active in the American Bar Association's efforts to curb gun violence.

There is considerable confusion and misunderstanding about the meaning of the Second Amendment and its relationship to the power of the federal government to enact laws regulating firearms in private hands. In fact, our concern about the widespread misunderstanding of the law in this area caused [Mississippi's] House of Delegates, in August 1994, to adopt a resolution calling on the legal profession to "... join and work with our counterparts in the medical, teaching, religious, civic, law enforcement and other professions, to ... educate the public and lawmakers regarding the meaning of the Second Amendment to the United States Constitution, to

David W. Clark, "Statement to the Subcommittee on the Constitution, Federalism and Property Rights," Committee on the Judiciary, United States Senate, September 23, 1998. Reproduced by permission.

make widely known the fact that the United States Supreme Court and lower federal courts have consistently, uniformly held that the Second Amendment to the United States Constitution right to bear arms is related to a well-regulated militia and that there are no federal constitutional decisions which preclude regulation of firearms in private hands."

No Confusion in the Law

Few issues have been more distorted and cluttered by misinformation than this one. We agree with the views of former Solicitor General (and Dean of Harvard Law School) Erwin N. Griswold, expressed in his November 4, 1990, *Washington Post* column, "Phantom Second Amendment Rights," that the debate then ongoing as to a proposed ban on assault weapons should spend little time on "the unsupportable claim that restrictions would violate the Second Amendment's right to keep and bear arms."

There is no confusion in the law itself. Federal and state court decisions in this century have been uniform in the view that the Second Amendment permits the exercise of broad power to limit private access to firearms by all levels of government. The strictest gun control laws in the nation have been upheld against Second Amendment challenge, including a ban on handguns imposed locally.

The Supreme Court enunciated in 1939 in *United States v. Miller* what almost sixty years later remains clearly the law of the land—namely, that the scope of the people's right to bear arms is qualified by the introductory phrase of the Second Amendment regarding the necessity of a "well regulated militia" for the "security of a free State." In *Miller*, the Court held that the "obvious purpose" of the Amendment was "to assure the continuation and render possible the effectiveness of . . ." the state militias and cautioned that the Amendment "must be interpreted and applied with that end in view."

The Militia in colonial times was not an ad hoc gathering of persons. The Militia was a creature of law, with appointed officers, and terms of service, that acted as a branch of government. Since today's "well regulated militia" does not use privately owned firearms, courts since *Miller* have unanimously held that regulation of such guns does not offend the Second Amendment. The Supreme Court has twice reaffirmed its view of the Second Amendment as expressed in *Miller*. In *Burton v. Sills* (1968), the Court dismissed, for want of a substantial federal question, a gun owner's appeal of a New Jersey Supreme Court holding that the Second Amendment permits regulation of firearms "so long as the regulation does not impair the active, organized militias of the states." Most recently, in *Lewis v. United States* (1980), the Court held that legislative restrictions on the use of firearms do not—for purposes of equal protection analysis—"trench upon any constitutionally protected liberties."

The lower federal courts have uniformly followed the interpretation of the Supreme Court. The absolutist view of the Second Amendment argued by some opponents of regulation of firearms has not been sustained by a single U.S. Supreme Court or lower federal court decision in our nation's history, while a series of U.S. Supreme Court and lower federal court decisions has uniformly upheld regulation of private arms. Throughout our nation's history, no legislation regulating the private ownership of firearms has been struck down on Second Amendment grounds. Congress should require those who make such broad claims about the inability of Congress to constitutionally regulate in this area to point to some court decision upholding such views.

Congress Must Decide

The fact that the Second Amendment permits federal regulation of firearms has allowed Congress in recent years to prevent the sale and manufacture of terrorist weapons undetectable to airport and public building security, to restrict sale and possession of fully automatic machine guns, to outlaw "cop-killer" bullets, and to ban sale and possession of military assault weapons. None of these measures has been overturned in the courts. In recent years, the gun industry has consistently chosen not to raise Second Amendment claims in court. As lawyers we know why. They cannot point to a single legitimate precedent to support their claims.

Moreover, the fact that the Second Amendment permits regulation of firearms does not mean, as the gun lobby implies, that Congress will abuse that power to prevent sporting uses of firearms, the purchase of guns for self-defense, or other legitimate uses of guns. This is not an "all or nothing" proposition. Rather, the question before Congress is where to draw the line to balance interests of gun owners and manufacturers with public safety and public order. In the case of military assault weapons, Congress made a public policy choice regarding the benefits of having such weapons in general circulation versus the horrible costs they can inflict upon an innocent citizenry.

Epidemic of Violence

Gun violence in the United States is a grave national problem. . . .

Firearms are overwhelmingly the instrument used in committing homicides in the United States and our homicide rate, especially for young persons, remains many times higher than the rest of the industrialized world. Worldwide statistics show that the epidemic of violence that has hit younger children in recent years is confined almost exclusively to the United States. . . .

The American Bar Association believes that the costs of gun violence to our society have become an enormous public burden. The Centers for Disease Control and leading health experts have conducted research, collected data, and published results regarding the nationwide cost of firearms injuries, and have shown that firearms injuries and death in the United States are at an epidemic level of occurrence. The dollar costs of medical care have become a significant contributor to health care costs nationwide. The cost to the public of paying for medical care and losses suffered as the result of firearms injuries and death is enormous. . . .

We urge Congress to take appropriate steps to regulate firearms to reduce the tragic carnage of gun-related deaths and injuries plaguing this country. The Constitution clearly permits such regulation, and the Second Amendment cannot be used as a reason for failing to adopt appropriate regulatory legislation.

Early Legal Scholars Supported an Individual Right to Bear Arms

Steven G. Bradbury, Howard C. Nielson Jr., and C. Kevin Marshall

In this selection from a memo intended to advise the attorney general of the United States, three U.S. attorneys argue that the right to bear arms was considered an individual right at the time of America's founding. The right to bear arms logically followed from the right to defend oneself and one's home; no government could infringe that right. The Second Amendment's purpose was not only to ensure the right to self-defense, but to ensure the liberty of the people from tyrannical government. Only an individual right to bear arms could guarantee such freedom, the authors conclude.

Steven G. Bradbury has served as principal deputy assistant attorney general, Howard C. Nielson Jr. as deputy assistant attorney general, and C. Kevin Marshall as acting deputy assistant attorney general.

In the generations immediately following its ratification, the three leading commentators to consider the Second Amendment each recognized that its right of the people to keep and bear arms belonged to individuals, not to States and not just to members of militias (whether of organized, select militia units or even of the citizen militia). Nearly all of the discussions of the antebellum [prior to the Civil War] courts, including in the leading cases, understood the right in the same way, whether they were considering the Second Amendment or similar provisions in state constitutions. This early under-

Steven G. Bradbury, Howard C. Nielson Jr., and C. Kevin Marshall, "Whether the Second Amendment Secures an Individual Right: Memorandum Opinion for the Attorney General," Office of the Attorney General, August 24, 2004.

standing of a personal right continued at least through Reconstruction. The modern alternative views of the Second Amendment did not take hold until 1905, well over a century after the Amendment had been ratified.

In the first few decades after the Second Amendment was drafted and ratified, each of the three leading commentators on the Constitution addressed it: St. George Tucker, William Rawle, and Joseph Story. Each agreed that it protects an individual right. Less prominent early commentators also concurred with this interpretation.

Tucker, a judge and law professor from Virginia, published in 1803 an edition of [William] Blackstone's *Commentaries* [*on the Laws of England*] to which he had added annotations and essays explaining the relation of American law, including the new Constitution, to England's. *Tucker's Blackstone* quickly became the leading American authority on both Blackstone and American law.

Right to Bear Arms Is a Natural Right

Tucker addressed the Second Amendment at several points. He first did so, repeatedly, in his introductory *View of the Constitution of the United States*. He tied the federal right, as Blackstone had the English one, to the individual, natural right of self-defense and to the freedom of the state. After quoting the Amendment, he wrote:

> This may be considered as the true palladium of liberty. . . . The right of self defence is the first law of nature: in most governments it has been the study of rulers to confine this right within the narrowest limits possible. Wherever standing armies are kept up, and the right of the people to keep and bear arms is, under any colour or pretext whatsoever, prohibited, liberty, if not already annihilated, is on the brink of destruction.

He condemned the use of the game laws in England as a pretext to disarm ordinary people—the "farmer, or inferior tradesman, or other person not qualified to kill game." And he grouped the Second Amendment right with those of the First, confirming that all belonged to individuals:

> If, for example, a law be passed by congress, prohibiting the free exercise of religion, according to the dictates, or persuasions of a man's own conscience; or abridging the freedom of speech, or of the press; or the right of the people to assemble peaceably, or to keep and bear arms; it would, in any of these cases, be the province of the judiciary to pronounce whether any such act were constitutional, or not; and if not, to acquit the accused . . .

An Individual Right

Second, in annotating Blackstone's description, in Book I, Chapter 1, of the individual English subject's right to have and use arms for self-defense, Tucker praised the Second Amendment "right of the people" for being "without any qualification as to their condition or degree, as is the case in the British government" (under England's Bill of Rights) and again denounced the game laws, by which "the right of keeping arms is effectually taken away from the people of England." Finally, in a note to one of Blackstone's (critical) discussions of the game laws, Tucker once more attacked them, because "it seems to be held" that no one but the very rich has "any right to keep a gun in his house" or "keep a gun for their defence," the result being that "the whole nation are completely disarmed, and left at the mercy of the government," and "the mass of the people" are kept "in a state of the most abject subjection." By contrast, "in America we may reasonably hope that the people will never cease to regard the right of keeping and bearing arms as the surest pledge of their liberty."

In all of these discussions, the right belonged to individuals—to persons availing themselves of the natural, individual "right of self defence," to the "accused" seeking judicial review of a violation of the Second Amendment, and to "the mass" of ordinary people able to defend themselves because protected by the Second Amendment from class-based pretexts for disarmament. Tucker understood both the English and American rights to arms to belong to individuals, and he thought the latter more secure and broad-based.

Nowhere did Tucker suggest that the right of the people to keep and bear arms depended on a person's enrollment and exercise in the citizen militia (much less his membership in an organized, select militia unit) or that it was a "right" that belonged to state governments. He did elsewhere, in discussing the Militia Clauses, point out that the Second Amendment eliminated "all room for doubt, or uneasiness" on whether the federal Government could prohibit States from simply providing arms for their militias (doubt he rightly found questionable given that the original Constitution left a concurrent arming power in the States). Tucker did not suggest here that he thought the Amendment had only this effect, and his other discussions confirm that he did not so understand it.

Restrictions on Congressional Power

William Rawle of Pennsylvania published his *View of the Constitution of the United States of America* in 1825, with a second edition appearing in 1829. After having turned down President Washington's offer to be the first attorney general, he had served in the Pennsylvania Assembly when it ratified the Bill of Rights. His commentary, like Tucker's, gained wide prominence.

Rawle analyzed the Second Amendment in a chapter entitled "Of the Restrictions on the Powers of Congress ... [,] Restrictions on the Powers of States and Security to *the Rights of Individuals*," by which he meant, respectively, Article I, Section 9; Article I, Section 10; and the first eight amendments of the Bill of Rights. He started with the Second Amendment's preface, giving to it, including the word "Militia," precisely the sense and significance that emerges from our analysis above, and making clear that the substantive right belonged to the ordinary citizen:

> In the second article, it is declared, that *a well regulated militia is necessary to the security of a free state*; a proposition from which few will dissent. Although in actual war, the services of regular troops are confessedly more valuable; yet, while peace prevails, and in the commencement of a war before a regular force can be raised, the militia form the palladium of the country. . . . That they should be well regulated, is judiciously added. . . . The duty of the state government is, to adopt such regulations as will tend to make good soldiers with the least interruptions of the ordinary and useful occupations of civil life. . . .
>
> The corollary, from the first position, is, that *the right of the people to keep and bear arms shall not be infringed.*
>
> The prohibition is general. No clause in the Constitution could by any rule of construction be conceived to give to congress a power to disarm the people. Such a flagitious [shameful] attempt could only be made under some general pretence by a state legislature. But if in any blind pursuit of inordinate power, either should attempt it, this amendment may be appealed to as a restraint on both.

Both Rawle's language—the Amendment's prohibition "is general" and protects the arms of "the people" —and his view of the Second Amendment as applying to the States and *restricting* their power indicate that he saw the right as individual, not as collective or quasi-collective. . . .

Rawle further explained the individual-right view's understanding of the Second Amendment preface when discussing the President's limited power to command the militia. Although not mentioning the Amendment expressly, he noted: "In a people permitted and accustomed to bear arms, we have the rudiments of a militia, which properly consists of armed citizens, divided into military bands, and instructed at least in part in the use of arms for the purposes of war." Thus, the "people" of the country, as individuals, keep and bear arms for private purposes; they also form the militia; and the former facilitates the latter, but only as a rudiment. That is why the individual right is a "corollary" from the need for a militia.

Arms Are a Check on Arbitrary Power

The same view appears in the influential 1833 *Commentaries on the Constitution of the United States* of Supreme Court Justice and law professor Joseph Story, as well as in his later *Familiar Exposition* of the Constitution. The *Commentaries* appeared first in a three-volume set and then, a few months later, in a one-volume abridgement by Story (the *Abridgement*).

Story devoted a chapter of his *Abridgement* to the Bill of Rights. Before turning to its provisions, he recounted the debate over whether to add one and identified several purposes, all related to individual rights: (1) to prevent powers granted to the government from being exercised in a way "dangerous to the people"; (2) as part of "the muniments [entitlements] of freemen, showing their title to protection," to ensure against an "extravagant or undue extention of" powers granted; and (3) to protect minorities. He then singled out those amendments that did not relate to judicial procedure (the First, Second, Third, Fourth, Eighth, Ninth, and Tenth) as those addressing "subjects properly belonging to a bill of rights."

With regard to the Second Amendment, he first explained the importance of the militia for "a free country," including as a check on "domestic usurpations of power," and the hazards "for a free people" of keeping up "large military establishments and standing armies in time of peace." He linked these policies to the right: "The right of the citizens to keep, and bear arms has justly been considered, as the palladium of the liberties of a republic; since it offers a strong moral check against the usurpation and arbitrary power of rulers; and will generally, even if these are successful in the first instance, enable the people to resist and triumph over them." In the unabridged version, he cited Tucker, Rawle, and the House of Representatives' first day of debate on the Amendment in support of this sentence.

By paraphrasing the "right of the people" as the "right of the citizens" —not of States or members of their militias—as well as by citing Tucker and Rawle's discussions (including borrowing from Tucker's "palladium" language), Story left no doubt that he considered the right to belong to individuals. He reinforced this point in an additional paragraph in the unabridged version, citing both Blackstone's discussion of the "similar provision" in England—clearly an individual right, as explained above—and Tucker's discussion of what Story called the "defensive privilege" there. In his *Familiar Exposition*, Story began his discussion of the Amendment with an even more explicit statement: "One of the ordinary modes, by which tyrants accomplish their purposes without resistance, is, by disarming the people, and making it an offence to keep arms, and by substituting a regular army in the stead of a resort to the militia."

Thus Story, like Tucker, Rawle, and others, recognized that the right that the Second Amendment secured was an individual one. He also saw, as they had, that this personal right was necessary for ensuring a well-regulated militia of the people. But he likewise recognized, consistent with the individual-right view, that such a right was not sufficient for ensuring such an entity, wondering how it would be "practicable to keep the people duly armed without some organization," and lamenting the decline of militia discipline.

The Individual-Right Interpretation of the Second Amendment Is Unfounded

Saul Cornell

The rise of the "individual-right" interpretation of the Second Amendment has attracted critics. This interpretation holds that the Second Amendment gives each individual the right to own and carry a weapon. Scholars holding the individual-right view note that at the time of the creation of the Constitution the militia was composed of every free citizen; therefore, the right to possess weapons applies to everyone.

To support this view, gun rights advocates turn to historical sources. In this essay, Ohio State history professor Saul Cornell says that these advocates are misrepresenting evidence. They practice what he calls "law office history" in trying to use the past to make their point. Such scholars often engage in selective use of quotes and exaggerate the meaning of writings advocating the individual-right interpretation, he claims. Rigorous historical scholarship, on the other hand, Cornell argues, involves a careful weighing of all pertinent evidence.

While [Susan] Sarandon, [Charlton] Heston, and others invoke the past in political debates over gun control,[1] judges and legal scholars also use history to try and determine what sorts of laws are compatible with the Second Amendment's protection for the right to keep and bear arms. No constitutional right is absolute, not even the right to free speech, since courts have upheld restrictions on pornography

---

1. Susan Sarandon is an actress and pro-gun-control activist. Charlton Heston is an actor and former president of The National Rifle Association.

Saul Cornell, "The Second Amendment Under Fire: The Uses of History and the Politics of Gun Control," History Matters: The U.S. Survey Course on the Web, http://historymatters.gmu.edu, January 2001. Reproduced by permission of the author.

and "fighting words." The debate over the Second Amendment pits supporters of an individual right to gun ownership against those who believe the Bill of Rights only protects the right of the people to maintain a well-regulated militia. Apart from a few Second Amendment absolutists, most supporters of the individual rights view believe that some restrictions on gun ownership are allowable. But such restrictions must meet a very high standard of constitutional scrutiny. In essence, to be legal a gun law must be narrowly tailored and it must be designed to accomplish a compelling state interest to avoid running afoul of the Second Amendment.

The second view, the collective rights interpretation, argues that the Bill of Rights provides no protection for an individual right to own guns. Such a right might exist under particular state constitutions, but the Second Amendment is about the militia and nothing else. Until quite recently judges and the authors of the casebooks used to train law students accepted the collective rights reading of *United States v. Miller* (1939). In that case the U.S. Supreme Court held that "in the absence of any evidence tending to show that possession or use of a 'shotgun having a barrel of less than eighteen inches in length' at this time has some reasonable relationship to the preservation or efficiency of a well regulated militia, we cannot say that the Second Amendment guarantees the right to keep and bear such an instrument." The consensus built around *Miller* has come under fire on several fronts. Some legal scholars argue that if one followed *Miller*'s logic there would be no constitutional right to own a hunting rifle, while military assault weapons would enjoy constitutional protection. Still others argue that in *Miller* the justices simply misread history and ignored the existence of a well established individual right to own guns.

Emerson v. United States: A New Test Case for Gun Control?

A new test case now working its way through the federal court system may change things entirely. The facts of the case are straightforward. Dr. Timothy Joe Emerson, a physician who had fallen on hard times, threatened his estranged wife's hairdresser boyfriend. Emerson's wife obtained a restraining order against her husband. When Emerson's wife went to his medical office, Emerson pulled out a 9 millimeter Berretta pistol and ordered his wife and four-year-old daughter to get off his property. Emerson was indicted under a federal statute that prohibits individuals under domestic violence restraining orders from being in possession of a weapon. At the time of his arrest Emerson had two 9 millimeter pistols, a military issue semiautomatic M1 carbine, a semiautomatic SKS assault rifle with a bayonet, and a semiautomatic M14. When Emerson's case came before Samuel Cummings, a Texas Federal Court judge, Emerson's court-appointed public defender argued that his client's Second Amendment rights had been violated. Judge Cummings agreed with the public defender and based his decision on recent legal scholarship on the Second Amendment that supports an individual rights interpretation of the Amendment. If *Emerson v. U.S.* (1999) comes before the Supreme Court [and it had not as of late 2006], it is possible that the Court might reject the previous finding of the *Miller* case entirely or reaffirm the collective rights view.

Cummings's decision in *Emerson* drew on a growing body of legal scholarship on the Second Amendment that supports the individual rights view. Although individual rights scholars have proclaimed that their interpretation is the new consensus, other legal scholars have rejected it. There is no disputing the fact that a number of prominent constitutional experts have been won over to the individual rights view. Most historians, however, reject the individual rights interpretation. How do we explain this sharp divide between legal scholars and historians? Much of the difference has to do with the problem of context. Much Second Amendment scholarship has taken the form of "law office history," a form of advocacy scholarship designed to influence the way courts decide constitutional questions. Legal scholarship influences the way briefs are written and may also be used by judges when deciding a case. For most historians the goal of scholarship is to reconstruct and understand the complexity of the past, not influence contemporary policy or jurisprudence. Sometimes historians do use their scholarship in a fashion similar to legal scholars. Yet, even for those historians interested in a useable past, one that can inspire or guide us, such scholarship must be judged by the same rules of evidence and argument that are used to evaluate any work of history.

Professional History vs. Law Office History

Perhaps the best way to illustrate the difference between law office history and the kind of history practiced by professional historians is to examine how the same source would be interpreted by both groups. Many legal scholars have interpreted Tench Coxe's "Remarks on the First Part of the Amendments to the Federal Constitution" (published under the pen name "A Pennsylvanian" in the Philadelphia *Federal Gazette*, June 18, 1789) to support the individual rights view of the Second Amendment. But analyzing Coxe's "Remarks" in their historical context raises significant challenges to the idea that they support an individual rights interpretation of the Second Amendment.

In June, 1789, when Coxe published his "Remarks," members of Congress were drafting a series of twelve amendments to the Constitution (which had been ratified in late 1788). Ten of these were ratified by the states and have become known as the Bill of Rights. Most of the provisions of the Bill of Rights protected individual liberties and were added to the Constitution to alleviate popular fears about a strong, centralized federal government. Some provisions of the Bill of Rights affirmed the rights of the states or the people in their collective capacity. Coxe was a prominent Federalist and had written several essays in defense of the Constitution as part of the spirited debates that had taken place in the press while it was being drafted and ratified.

Lawyer Stephen Halbrook, a leading modern spokesperson for individual rights legal theorists, describes Coxe's "Remarks" as "the most complete exposition of the Bill of Rights to be published during its ratification period." Coxe himself described his essay in rather different terms. "I have," he wrote James Madison, "taken an hour from my present Engagements, which on account of my absence are greater than usual, and have thrown together a few remarks upon the first part of the Resolutions." Halbrook may be technically correct that Coxe did comment on all of the proposed amendments before Congress, but one wonders how much weight to attribute to a hastily written essay.

Exaggerated Evidence

To support his claim that Coxe's view of the Second Amendment captures the intent of those who framed and ratified it, Halbrook claims that "Coxe's defense of the amendments was widely reprinted. A search of the literature of the time reveals that no writer disputed or contradicted Coxe's analysis." Actually, Coxe's essay appeared three times. In 1790 there were 84 newspapers in America, which means that Coxe's essay was ignored by more than 95% of the press. It is hard to see how this sort of evidence could prove that Coxe's essay was representative of widely held views or that it reached a particularly wide audience. Nor can one infer much from the fact that no one bothered to refute Coxe. The absence of a rebuttal might just as easily signify indifference as acceptance. The most reasonable conclusion to draw is that Coxe's essay was simply not very influential.

Another gun rights scholar, Don Kates, asserts that Coxe's essay was "authoritative—by virtue of having received Madison's imprimatur." This view was endorsed by another individual rights legal scholar, Glenn Harlan Reynolds, who wrote that "James Madison approved of Coxe's construction of the Second Amendment in a letter to Coxe dated June 24, 1789." But Madison never specifically commented on Coxe's discussion of the Second Amendment. As historian Jack Rakove notes, "Madison did not discuss the substance or merits of Coxe's interpretation of particular rights." What Madison did do was praise Coxe for defending the Bill of Rights in print, a move which Madison felt would have "a healing tendency."

But what exactly did Coxe have to say about the Second Amendment in his "Remarks"? Here is what Coxe wrote:

> As civil rulers, not having their duty to the people duly before them, may attempt to tyrannize, and as the military forces which must be occasionally raised to defend our country, might pervert their power to the injury of their fellow-citizens, the people are confirmed by the next article in their right to keep and bear their private arms.

Supporters of the individual rights view have focused on the fact that Coxe asserted that "the people are confirmed by the next article in their right to keep and bear their private arms." While at first glance this would seem to provide proof of an individual right, it is not clear in what capacity the people's private arms are protected. Are they protected as private citizens or are they protected because as militiamen citizens were expected to provide their own weapons for militia duty? Coxe's statement ultimately tells us little about how people understood the individual or collective nature of the right to keep and bear arms in the late-eighteenth century.

Serious Errors of Fact and Interpretation

Political and legal debates over the meaning of the Second Amendment will continue at rallies, in legislative halls, in the media, and in courtrooms throughout the United States. And all such debates will continue to rely on conflicting understandings of the past. Although the new individual rights scholarship on the Second Amendment has attracted some support among legal scholars, historians have uncovered serious errors of fact and interpretation in this body of scholarship. With more rigorous historical research it is possible that the balance may shift to the individual rights view. For the moment, however, the claim that the Second Amendment was originally understood to protect an individual right to gun ownership remains historically unproven and politically contested.

THE
HISTORY
OF
ISSUES

CHAPTER 3

Gun Control in the 1960s: Beginning of the Controversy

Chapter Preface

Gun control was a minor issue in the public consciousness until the 1960s. That decade of highly publicized urban and political turmoil led to increased public awareness of gun violence. By the end of the decade, Congress had passed a major federal gun control law, but a strong lobby in opposition to any sort of gun regulation had also formed.

The first calls for gun control came in 1963, immediately after President John F. Kennedy was assassinated by a gunman using a cheap mail-order rifle. Connecticut senator Thomas J. Dodd proposed outlawing some mail-order weapons and strengthening licensing requirements for firearms dealers. The National Rifle Association (NRA) instigated a public campaign to stop the legislation, and the proposed laws were not passed.

However, urban riots, rising crime rates, and continuing political assassinations created a climate in which gun control eventually passed Congress. Civil disturbances broke out in Los Angeles, Detroit, and other cities. Violent crime in general was increasing in American cities. Probably most important from a gun control perspective, however, was the rash of assassinations in the 1960s. They did not stop with Kennedy in 1963. Black nationalist activist Malcolm X was killed in 1966. Civil rights leader Martin Luther King Jr. was slain in April 1968, and Senator Robert F. Kennedy was killed while campaigning for president two months later in June 1968. After this last assassination Congress passed the Gun Control Act of 1968. This measure prohibited drug users and convicted criminals from purchasing handguns and outlawed the sale of mail-order rifles and shotguns.

The opposition to gun control did not disappear, however. The NRA, a formerly moderate group that actually helped draft some of the 1960s gun control legislation, experienced a grassroots revolt. Hard-liners such as Harlon Bronson Carter, the head of the NRA's legislative affairs institute, would not accept the compromises allowed by previous NRA leaders. Carter and his faction were effectively defeated in internal struggles over the 1968 act. Their support among the rank-and-file NRA members grew, however, and they managed to gain effective control of the organization in 1975. The hard-liners have controlled the NRA ever since.

Stricter Gun Regulation Is Necessary

Tom Batman

The assassination of John F. Kennedy in 1963, coupled with rising crime rates in American cities, touched off a debate about gun control and gun registration in the United States. In this 1964 Saturday Review *article, writer Tom Batman points out the need for handgun registration.*

At the time this article was written, there were very few gun control laws. The most significant was a law prohibiting the transportation of certain types of guns across state lines. In 1964 only seven states had any sort of registration requirement for gun owners. Batman notes new statistics showing a rise in gun violence and concludes that handgun control is urgently needed. He recommends that readers contact their congressional representative in support of stricter gun laws.

An automobile is an agent of transportation. Even though it can kill, it is not made for this express purpose. Every citizen who owns one is required to register it. No one makes any fuss about it; it seems a reasonable thing to do.

A gun is an agent of death. It is made for one express purpose—to kill. There is no national law that says that every citizen who owns one is required to register it. What's more, whenever the subject is mentioned, a great outcry is made about constitutional rights. Gun registration is not recognized as a protection to the citizen.

What accounts for this inconsistency? Do gun owners who are not currently registered fear persecution or invasion of privacy? Do they fear that they will somehow become publicly linked with the criminal element of our society? Or do vested interests feel that their business and profits will be harmed by registration?

New Statistics Show Need for Gun Control

At the time of the death of President Kennedy, this subject was hotly debated. Today, the smoke has died down. This is unfortunate. New statistics indicate that it should again be scrutinized and that we cannot afford to let it die by inattention or be glossed over by the passage of time.

In his report to the House Subcommittee on Apropriations in January of this year [1964], J. Edgar Hoover, director of the FBI [Federal Bureau of Investigation], revealed some thought-provoking figures. For one thing, they indicate that the problem now is not "I didn't know it was loaded." It is far more serious, said Mr. Hoover. "We are living in an age where guns are being used in murders, robberies, and many other vicious crimes." To be specific: 8,400 people were killed willfully in the United States in 1962 (latest figures available). More than half of these killings (54 per cent) were with the use of firearms, and of those killings 70 per cent were perpetrated with handguns such as revolvers.

Mr. Hoover states that the basic objection raised to gun registration is the argument (with which he does not agree) that under the Constitution one is allowed to keep and bear arms. We must support the Constitution, but not blindly, especially in the face of drastic changes in conditions. Everyone who knows American history knows that everyone in early days *had* to carry a gun—there were no police.

The American People Support Gun Registration

I suspect that our most honored patriots—fierce lovers of freedom such as Thomas Jefferson, George Washington, and

Andrew Jackson—would today endorse the idea of gun registration. To own an unregistered gun today is to act against freedom, not for it.

The following points were made on the *CBS Reports* telecast of June 10 [1964] on *Murder and the Right to Bear Arms*: Only seven states require a license to buy a gun, and although a recent Gallup Poll showed that 78 per cent of Americans are in favor of some kind of registration, the opposition is such that apparently there is little prospect that the measure will be enacted.

Under these conditions, then, could there be other, hidden reasons for opposing registration—logical or otherwise—reasons that cannot be publicly or directly stated? What are the *legitimate* groups that might lobby against—or be opposed to—this issue, out of what they consider to be a reasonable position?

Handguns vs. Rifles

It would seem that the distinguishing feature of special interest here is hunting (with guns, of course). None of the people I know who are interested in hunting are unpatriotic; in fact, they are most likely to be what we call "red-blooded" citizens. Those who are opposed to gun registration are misguided, in my opinion, perhaps because they sense a vague threat of some kind of control over their vocation or avocation, as the case may be.

The plain fact of the matter is that people don't ordinarily go hunting with handguns; they hunt with rifles. And people don't murder, generally, with rifles; they murder with handguns. The statistics are indisputable. For this reason, gun and ammunition companies, editors of hunting magazines, writers of newspaper hunting columns, men who sell hunting licenses, and hunters themselves should take an active part in lobbying not against registration of arms, but for it.

It was only natural for the framers of the Constitution, in their circumstances, to feel that their fellow men should be allowed to keep and bear arms. This was as necessary in those days as the existence and effectiveness of the police force is in these days. But today the lack of strict legislation controlling firearms causes unnecessary difficulties to the police in the execution of their duty.

Mr. Hoover has pointed out that in the period from 1960 to 1962, 113 law enforcement officers were killed as a result of criminal action. Of those 113 murders, 109 were committed with guns, the majority of which were handguns.

In other words, many of the unregistered weapons we apathetically allow to be sold without restriction are turned against the very forces we rely on for maintaining law and order.

Comparing Dallas and New York City

Is this a sensible position for us to take? Consider the differences related by Mr. Hoover in the cases of New York and Dallas with respect to gun laws. There are no gun laws in Dallas, although they do have some state firearms control laws; the laws concerning firearms in New York are rather strict but even those require strengthening (new legislation is pending).

In 1962 there were 507 murders in New York City, and only 28 per cent were committed with a gun; in the same year, there were 103 murders in Dallas, and 67 per cent of them were committed with a gun. In 1963 the figures are even more disparate. In New York City, 25 per cent of murders were committed with guns; in Dallas, 72 per cent were committed with guns.

Clearly, stricter laws are urgently needed.

What can the concerned citizen do about this? Mr. Hoover believes that there should be a uniform statute enacted at state levels and supported by various civic organizations. The citizen can support Mr. Hoover's suggestion—write to Congressmen, enlist the aid of civic organizations, persuade friends to do the same thing. He can press the issue at both the federal and the state levels, knowing that the government will act when the public becomes sufficiently aroused. . . .

We need new laws regulating firearms, and we can bring them to fruition if we do something about it.

Gun Control Violates the Rights of Citizens

Frank S. Meyer

In this 1968 magazine article, conservative writer Frank S. Meyer argues that the rush to implement gun control is mistaken both from a practical policy standpoint and from a constitutional standpoint. As a policy, gun control will not reduce the amount of illegitimate violence because those who commit such violence do not obey laws. However, such laws will interfere with legitimate acts of violence, such as a homeowner defending his or her property from intruders.

From a legal standpoint, Meyer sees gun control as unconstitutional. The Second Amendment is clear that no infringement on the right to bear arms is allowed. While proponents of gun control argue that regulation is not infringement, Meyer counters with the example of New York's Sullivan law, which he says has made it nearly impossible for law-abiding residents of New York State to obtain firearms.

Frank S. Meyer was a conservative writer and thinker whose best-known work is In Defense of Freedom: A Conservative Credo.

Since Adam ate the apple, the per capita quantum of violence and potential violence in human society has remained, century in and century out, reasonably constant. Indeed, the third person in the world[1] killed the fourth—or, if you prefer more secular images, primitively there was always present "continual fear and danger of violent death; and the life of man, solitary, poor, nasty, brutish, and short" [Thomas Hobbes].

1. Meyer is referring to the Biblical Story of Cain, the son of Adam and Eve, killing his brother Abel.

Moral Authority and Force Control Violence

What has made the difference between the quantum [amount] of potential violence and actual violence has been the power of the moral authority of civilizations to inspire the members of society, and the firmness with which force has been exerted in defense of civilizations against external and internal barbarians. Against external barbarians, sometimes the moral authority of a great civilization has played a part, but primarily it has been force which has held the *limes*.[2] Against internal barbarians, the problem has been more mixed, since a civilization with sufficient moral authority tends to civilize its internal barbarians.

The abysmal ignorance of history, as of the elements of political philosophy, that characterizes so much of the political and intellectual leadership of the United States today is all that can explain, although it does not excuse, the torrent of nonsense about "violence" with which we have been assailed these past days and weeks and months. The simple knee-jerk reactions that pass for high political wisdom might be understandable in a local official of the League of Women voters; they are proclamations of bankruptcy when they come from men of supposed political or intellectual sophistication.

Violence is bad? Of course: then let us do away with it. Problem; solution: instant Utopia. Guns kill people? Put government control on guns: domestic peace in our time.

Fallacies of Pro-Gun Control Arguments

Despite its appealing simplicity, this enthymeme[3] conceals a double fallacy. In the first place, violence is not always evil *per se*. In the public sphere it is morally legitimate when employed to resist or overthrow tyranny. In the private sphere it is equally legitimate when employed against criminal incursion upon life or property. For the latter purpose it may fall

2. The *limes* (pronounced LEE-mehs), Latin for "boundary," were the defended borders that separated the Roman Empire from the Germanic barbarians.
3. An enthymeme is a logical argument with some of its premises left unstated.

into desuetude in times when, unlike our own, the constituted authorities are able to keep crime and riot under control. But it is always a residual right, and in times like ours it becomes the citizen's duty to use violence when necessary in his own defense and the defense of his family.

The second fallacy is that weapons or the accessibility of weapons creates violence. Violence, for good or ill, arises from the souls of men. Gun control would have no more effect ultimately upon the quantum of domestic violence than disarmament agreements have had upon the prevalence of warfare. Indeed, in the one case as in the other, the logical effect is only to strengthen the bad guys and weaken the good guys. It was Nazi Germany that was armed, it was Britain and the United States that were disarmed, in 1939. If gun-control legislation at any level were to be enacted in this country, it would be the criminals, the rioters, the insurrectionists, who would find illegal means of procuring weapons; it would be the solid citizens who would be disarmed.

These are the considerations, derived from a philosophical understanding of the nature of man and from practical experience, that make nonsense of the hysterical clamor for gun control now emanating from the serried megaphones of the Establishment. It is a clamor that might be ignored if the basic law of the land were still respected by the judiciary, if the Constitution had not become a paper document to be manipulated into its opposite by the Warren Court.[4] The Founding Fathers, whose wisdom was based upon theory and experience, tried almost 200 years years ago to defend the United States against such mischievous incitations to tyranny and crime as are invited by a disarmed citizenry. Boldly and unequivocally, the First Congress and the states, in the Second Amendment to the Constitution (Article II of the Bill of

4. The Earl Warren–led Supreme Court, 1953–1969, made several liberal, landmark decisions and was accused of "judicial activism" by conservatives.

Rights), proclaimed that "the right of the people to keep and bear arms shall not be infringed."

Regulating Guns Will Lead to Total Ban

The constitutional principle is strong and sweeping, so strong and sweeping that even the present Supreme Court, one hopes, will not be able to work its sinuous way around it—should Congress prove to be so subject to utopian pressure as to pass legislation defying it. The key word is "infringe," and there can be no doubt in common sense or in law that any proposals for registration are direct infringements of the free citizen's right to keep and bear arms. If I may paraphrase an old maxim: the power to regulate is the power to destroy. The patently unconstitutional Sullivan Act in New York State has shown, in its administration over the years, that registration of firearms (in this case of concealable weapons) has made it next to impossible for anyone legally to possess such arms. Criminals and insurrectionists, of course, get hold of them easily. Even the prohibition of sales by mail, while it is less integrally objectionable than registration, seems to be of doubtful constitutionality.

An unarmed citizenry is potentially the victim, first of anarchy, then of tyranny and totalitarianism. The present campaign to infringe the right to keep and bear arms is a utopian assault upon the freedom of American citizens—an assault scornful of the testimony of history, the counsels of morality, and the express mandate of the Constitution.

The Number of Handguns Must Be Reduced

George D. Newton Jr. and Franklin E. Zimring

Some policy makers thought the Gun Control Act of 1968 did not go far enough in restricting or regulating gun ownership. The gun violence experienced by Americans that year—such as the assassinations of Martin Luther King Jr. and Robert F. Kennedy and gunplay during urban riots—prompted a report by the staff of a government commission looking into violence in America. This excerpt from the 1970 report lays out further gun control measures that the commission believed would sharply reduce the number of handguns, and thus the level of violence, in America.

Some of the recommendations are fairly radical. For example, the authors state frankly that they wish to make a dramatic cut in the number of handguns on the streets of America by instituting strict testing and licensing rules. Some of the recommendations have been carried out in weakened form, however, such as criminal background checks for gun purchasers.

George D. Newton Jr. was the director for the Commission on the Causes and Prevention of Violence and is on the board of Handgun Control Inc. Franklin E. Zimring is William G. Simon Professor of Law at the University of California–Berkeley School of Law.

It can surprise no one that high rates of gun violence are connected with high rates of handgun ownership. When the number of handguns increases, gun violence increases, and where there are fewer guns, there is less gun violence.

If there were fewer handguns in this country, the knife and other weapons might replace the gun as instruments of

George D. Newton Jr. and Franklin E. Zimring, *Firearms and Violence in American Life: A Staff Report Submitted to the National Commission on the Causes and Prevention of Violence.* Washington, DC: Government Printing Office [1970], pp. 139–48.

violence. Even so, deaths and injuries would be reduced because a gun attack is five times as deadly as an attack with another weapon.

Reducing the Number of Handguns

The stockpile of handguns in this country is a legacy of traditional American attitudes toward firearms and decades of lax firearms control. Yet, the handgun in the house generally creates more danger than safety. The use of handguns for target shooting can be accommodated without such a stockpile of guns, and the handgun is unimportant as a hunting weapon. At the same time, civil disorder, racial tension, and fear of crime are turning our nation into an armed camp and have increased the role of firearms in violence. The vicious circle of Americans arming themselves to protect against other armed Americans must be broken. Finding effective and appropriate methods of reducing gun violence must be recognized as a national problem.

We have concluded that the only sure way to reduce gun violence is to reduce sharply the number of handguns in civilian hands in this country. We recognize this will be a massive and expensive task. But, the price is one that we should be prepared to pay. . . .

We submit the following recommendations with regard to public education, research, and legislation.

Public Education

Public education programs to inform Americans fully about the role of firearms in accidents, crime, and other forms of violence; a publicity campaign to reduce the number of loaded guns in American homes.

As symbols of our frontier tradition, toys for our children, and props for our movies and television, firearms are so commonplace to Americans that we seldom pause to reflect on their impact on our lives. Our casual attitude toward firearms may be shaken temporarily when tragedy strikes close to home or when the nation as a whole is aroused by a sensational act of gun violence. But Americans do not know the whole story of gun misuse in this country.

An information program is necessary to secure broad public support for meaningful firearms legislation and to encourage the safe and responsible use of firearms. Only after we know the risks to ourselves, our families, and our friends can we appreciate the need for legislation and for voluntary measures to eliminate the loaded gun from the home. If a citizen elects to own a firearm, he must understand the duties and responsibilities of such ownership and the safest methods of handling and storing firearms in his home or business. In addition to reappraising his own attitude toward keeping firearms in his home, each American must also appreciate how the security of our society is affected by millions of guns in millions of homes.

We urge in particular that the National Rifle Association and other private organizations devoted to hunting and sport shooting be enlisted with interested citizens and the media to assist in pointing out the dangers of loaded firearms in the home and the need for meaningful firearms legislation. . . .

Federal Legislation

Efforts to obtain uniform state firearms laws through voluntary action of the states have proven unsuccessful. We recommend a federal law establishing minimum federal standards for state firearms control systems. Within 3 years each state would enact a firearms control system meeting the federal standards or a federally administered system based on these standards will be established within that state. Federal guidelines to maximize consistency in interpreting the federal standards should be issued, although each state would be able to adjust its system to meet the federal standards in light of local conditions. Any state failing to enact a firearms law meeting federal standards would be subject to the establishment of a federal firearms control system within its borders. . . .

We recommend a national standard of restrictive handgun licensing to reduce substantially the 24 million handguns now in civilian hands in this country and thereby reduce the toll of gun violence. This handgun licensing system should be national in scope because the problem is national, and because a nonexistent or ineffective control system in one state makes it difficult for neighboring states to control gun violence. Yet, different states have different cultural patterns and crime problems, and handgun laws must vary somewhat in accordance with these differences. We recommend, therefore, that federal legislation establish minimum standards for handguns and allow the states some flexibility in adapting these standards to local conditions.

Under state-administered restrictive licensing systems, applicants would have to establish both their eligibility to possess and a particular need for a handgun and pass a test designed to determine whether they know how to use and safely store a handgun.

The objective of this state-administered national system would be to reduce the number of privately owned handguns in this country to a necessary minimum. All those who are not issued licenses and who must give up their handguns would be duly compensated.

Standards for State Handgun Laws

Federal law should prescribe the following minimum standards for state handgun laws:

1. All handgun owners and purchasers of handgun ammunition must be licensed. Licenses may be issued only to those who establish a need for such a firearm. Although need would be determined separately by each state, federal guidelines can encourage consistency. For instance, police officers, security guards, and some re-

tail merchants should qualify for handgun licenses. Normal household protection would not constitute sufficient need. Under such guidelines, the number of legally held handguns would be reduced to about 10 percent or less of the present 24 million.

2. Handgun licenses will be denied to persons convicted of or under indictment for crimes of violence, fugitives, narcotics addicts, mental incompetents and defectives, and minors under 21.

3. A safety test will be required before issuance of a license.

4. Firearms dealers will be regulated to insure that they sell handguns or ammunition only to persons with licenses. Dealers and individuals intending to sell or transfer handguns will be required to submit reports on all such transactions and wait 20 days before delivering the gun to the transferee; during this period, the state will verify that it is the license holder who intends to acquire a handgun. No such report will be required for sales of ammunition. Pawnshops will be prohibited from dealing in handguns or ammunition.

5. The license program will be administered by a state agency without discrimination as to sex, or religion.

6. Licensed handgun owners will be required to supply information on each handgun they own and to notify police promptly if a handgun is stolen or lost. A system of periodic auditing of licensed handgun owners to insure that they still own the handguns licensed to them will be administered by a state agency.

7. A federally financed program to purchase handguns from private citizens and to grant amnesty to persons who relinquish illegally owned handguns will be administered by a state agency.

Additional Recommendations

In order to obtain the maximum benefits from the foregoing
... proposals, we also recommend:

1. Establishment of a federal firearms agency to accumulate
   and store firearms information obtained by state and
   local firearms agencies and to act as a clearinghouse of
   firearms information for federal, state, and local law
   enforcement agencies. The director of this agency
   might also be empowered to supervise state firearms
   systems to insure fair administration that does not dis-
   criminate on the basis of race or other unlawful
   grounds. A federal review system could also be provided to allow aggrieved parties recourse through the
   federal courts, on either their own initiative or that of
   the U.S. Department of Justice.

2. The Gun Control Act of 1968 bans imports of guns that
   are not suited for sporting purposes. This ban should
   be extended to firearms of domestic manufacture, ex-
   cepting only the manufacture of handguns for use by
   law enforcement agencies and licensed owners.

3. Federal firearms laws should be amended to eliminate
   the possibility of firearms dealers transferring to non-
   residents by renting guns with a high security deposit
   that is subsequently forfeited. In addition, licensed federal firearms dealers should be strictly policed to eliminate all but legitimate dealers. Licensed dealers should
   be required to maintain security procedures to minimize theft of firearms, particularly during civil disor-
   ders.

4. Public and private campaigns should be fostered in
   states and cities to encourage persons to turn in un-
   wanted guns. Such turn-ins could be coordinated with
   occasional amnesty days when illegally owned handguns could be turned in without penalty.

5. Public and private shooting clubs should be allowed to store handguns suitable for sporting purposes and to permit target shooters to use them on the premises.

6. The FBI should revise its crime reporting system to obtain a statistical breakdown of crimes involving firearms by type of weapon—handgun rifle, or shotgun.

7. Customs regulations should be amended to require written declaration of each firearm brought into this country from abroad and impounding of such firearms until legality of ownership is established.

The National Rifle Association Hardens Its Opposition to Gun Control

Osha Gray Davidson

*In the following excerpt Osha Gray Davidson describes the trans-
formation of the largest gun rights organization in America, the
National Rifle Association (NRA). The NRA was formed in
1871 as an organization devoted to marksmanship and firearms
safety. With congressional pressure for federal gun control growing in the wake of the assassination of President John F. Kennedy
in 1963, the leaders of the NRA were willing to compromise. After passage of the Gun Control Act of 1968, they were even con-
templating abandoning efforts at influencing Congress. The leaders planned to shift the emphasis of the group even more toward
recreational activities such as wilderness survival and marksmanship competition.*

*One man, however, a former Border Patrol official named
Harlon Carter, almost single-handedly reversed this course.
Carter and a hard-line group of allies battled fiercely against
what they saw as surrender on the part of NRA officials. In
1977, after suffering an initial defeat, the hard-liners were able
to win control of the organization. Since that time, the NRA has
been a fierce and effective opponent of virtually all gun control
legislation. Davidson is an author who specializes in environmental journalism. This selection is taken from his book* Under
Fire: The NRA and the Battle for Gun Control.

In the long history of the National Rifle Association, Harlon
Bronson Carter looms as a singular, towering figure—at
least as important as [NRA founder] William Conant Church,

Osha Gray Davidson, *Under Fire: The NRA and the Battle for Gun Control.* New York:
Henry Holt and Company, 1993, pp. 28–36. Reproduced by permission of Henry Holt
and Company, LLC.

and certainly more so to the modern gun group. Even macho hunters grow misty-eyed at the mere mention of his name. To the NRA faithful, Harlon Carter is Moses, George Washington, and John Wayne rolled into one.

Part of Carter's personal appeal was due to his striking physical appearance. Above piercing ice-blue eyes, he kept his bald head as polished as the nose cone of an ICBM [intercontinental ballistic missile]. (His detractors sometimes referred to him as Ol' Bullet Head.) If he seemed taller than he actually was, perhaps that was because of his barrel chest and massive arms; Carter looked like a Rodin statue come to life. . . .

If there was one thing Harlon Carter could not stand, it was gun control. The very idea of the government coming between a law-abiding citizen and his or her choice of firearms sent Carter into fits. Sweat would break out on his already glossy dome, and his face would turn as red as freshly butchered game.

You don't stop crime by attacking guns—he'd thunder, his blue eyes ablaze—*you stop crime by stopping criminals!*

It was bad enough when East Coast liberals talked such foolishness. You couldn't expect any better from them. But when, [retired general Franklin] Orth, a military man *and the head of the NRA for chrissake*, started spouting that drivel, that was heresy!

After 1968, things continued to go downhill as far as Carter was concerned. The NRA leadership steered the group further away from legislative issues and back toward hunting and conservation. In 1975 all responsibility for lobbying was handed over to a new, quasi-independent wing (it was on a longer leash, at any rate) called the Institute for Legislative Action (ILA), with Harlon Carter at the helm. Carter was continually complaining that he wasn't given the resources to do the job necessary. In point of fact, the organization was becoming more and more polarized on the issue of exactly how much of a job *was* necessary.

If Carter and his faction of hard-liners were upset by the leadership's penny-pinching when it came to lobbying, they were infuriated when they learned what else the old guard had planned for their beloved NRA.

Controversy over a New Shooting Range

The new controversy centered around the NRA's annual shooting competition, which had been moved from Creedmoor, Long Island, to Camp Perry, Ohio, some years earlier. In the late 1960s, the tournaments were still being paid for by U.S. tax dollars funneled through the army's Division of Civilian Marksmanship (DCM). The matches, which now cost $3 million a year and required the aid of 5,000 army troops, seemed like a colossal waste of resources to Senator Edward Kennedy (who was, admittedly, no friend of the NRA)—especially at a time when the Vietnam War was gobbling up the nation's treasury. Kennedy moved to have the military drop the program.

Although he wasn't immediately successful, the leaders of the NRA saw the handwriting on the wall and decided it would be prudent to begin looking for an alternative site, should they be denied access to Camp Perry at some time in the future. A search committee was formed, and eventually it selected a suitable location in a beautiful and wild section of northern New Mexico. The NRA bought 37,000 acres of land there.

There was some grumbling among the hard-liners about the decision to spend a lot of money for a new rifle range when the ILA was still trying to scrimp by, but the matter wasn't seen as being too important. At least not until the hard-liners learned that the old guard had bigger plans for the National Shooting Center outside of Raton, New Mexico. It wouldn't just be a place to shoot. With so many acres at their disposal it made good sense to add some other, related, activities like camping and wilderness survival training; conservation education; environmental awareness. The NRA could teach all types of outdoor skills there. That being the case— mused the old guard—why call it a National *Shooting* Center at all? Maybe just the National *Outdoor* Center.

This was treason. To the hard-liners, the name change was a bullet aimed at the very soul of the gun organization. Maybe they could hold *bird-watching* classes, the hard-liners sneered. National *Outdoor* Center? Why stop there? Hell, why not just change the name from the National Rifle Association to the National Outdoor Association? Immediately, a rumor swept through the hard-liner ranks that at least one powerful board member was considering just such a proposal.

The "Weekend Massacre"

Harlon Carter had heard enough. Always a man of action, he now decided that the time had come to do something. He was in the midst of plotting a palace coup when, late one after-noon in November 1976, the old guard got the drop on the former Border Patrol agent and fired twenty-four NRA em-ployees—most of them members of Carter's hard-liner group. The firings, which came on a Saturday, would be forever re-membered by NRA veterans as the "Weekend Massacre." Al-though Carter himself was too powerful a figure to terminate, he resigned in protest over the mass firings. The members of the old guard breathed a sigh of relief. With Carter and his foot soldiers gone they could get back to their work of mak-ing the NRA into the nation's preeminent outdoors organiza-tion. In furtherance of this goal, they announced plans to sell the headquarters building in Washington, D.C., and move all operations to Colorado Springs, not far from the National Outdoor Center. That might make the task of lobbying Con-gress more difficult, but then legislative action was no longer an NRA priority.

Six months later, the NRA's executive vice president (and leader of the old guard), General Maxwell Rich stood on a stage at the Cincinnati Convention-Exposition Center and welcomed members to the group's annual meeting. This was to be a time of healing, hoped Rich—of pulling together, of forgetting the fights of the past few years and getting on with the business of building a stronger NRA.

Harlon Carter and his brigade of hard-liners had other plans for the meeting, however. Like the marines hitting the beach at Anzio, the group of hard-liners—calling themselves the Federation for NRA—took over the meeting, using parliamentary procedure as their heavy artillery. Coordinating their moves by means of walkie-talkies, the men introduced several changes in the group's bylaws that would diminish the power in the hands of the elected officials and give the membership more say in the organization's affairs.

The Hard-Liners Emerge Victorious

The old guard never knew what hit them. The membership overwhelmingly voted for the changes. Plans to move the group's headquarters to Colorado Springs were put on hold, as were those for the hated National Outdoor Center. And then the members overwhelmingly voted against nearly every top NRA official, one by one. When the smoke cleared, leaders of the Federation for NRA occupied every position of power.

Minutes before his elevation to the supreme post of executive vice president, the commander of the federation forces mounted the podium at the front of the hall and addressed the cheering crowd below. "Beginning in this place and at this hour, this period in NRA history is finished," Harlon Carter proclaimed.

Carter was right. The Cincinnati Revolt (as the episode became known) changed forever the face of the NRA. Under Carter's robust leadership, and with the help of his chief lieutenant, Neal Knox (who took over as head of the ILA), the NRA became more than a rifle club. It became the Gun Lobby. Forget about hunting clinics, forget target shooting; those activities were now sideshows, mere extras. The new NRA would be devoted single-mindedly—and proud of the fact—to the proposition that Americans and their guns must never, *never* be parted.

Testifying before Congress in a calm but steel-edged voice, his blue eyes fixed directly on the committee chairman, Carter gave his enemies fair warning.

"We are," he told them, "in this game for keeps."

CHAPTER 4

Gun Control Legislation in the 1980s and 1990s

Chapter Preface

As in the 1960s, political violence played a pivotal role in the debate over gun control in the 1980s. The assassination attempt on President Ronald Reagan in 1981 was an important event in the history of gun control, not so much because it prompted calls for new legislation, but because it motivated Sarah Brady to join the movement. Brady's husband James, Reagan's press secretary, was shot in the head during the attack and left severely disabled. This tragedy prompted Sarah to get involved with Handgun Control Inc., a major gun control organization, and to lobby hard for new gun laws.

Despite Brady's efforts, gun control advocates were not especially successful during the 1980s. In fact, they experienced some key legislative defeats. A bill to ban armor-piercing "cop-killer" bullets failed. Moreover, the Gun Owners Protection Act, also known as the McClure-Volkmer Act, succeeded in gutting many of the provisions of the 1968 Gun Control Act. Both of these votes were victories for the National Rifle Association (NRA), the nation's largest gun rights organization.

The tide turned for the gun control movement in the 1990s. With the Democratic president Bill Clinton in office, gun control advocates operated in a friendlier political climate. Also important was increased support from organized law enforcement organizations, which were growing more skeptical of the NRA's no-compromise stand on guns. These conditions allowed gun control advocates—led by Sarah Brady—to bring about the passage of two key pieces of legislation.

The first important victory was the Brady Bill, part of a larger crime bill passed in 1994. It mandated a waiting period and background check for any handgun purchase. In addition, it set up a nationwide system for tracking criminal records so that gun dealers would be able to determine if a purchaser was eligible to buy a weapon. Although aspects of this law were later overturned, the system of waiting periods and federal background checks remains intact.

A second victory was the ban on assault weapons, also part of the 1994 crime bill. The law appealed to people who had been shocked by several instances of multiple shootings in which the criminal(s) used a military-type weapon. Detractors said that this law did not clearly define assault weapons and was a symbolic rather than a serious effort to control crime. After all, assault weapons were used in less than 1 percent of crimes.

Despite being defeated on the Brady Bill and assault weapons ban, the National Rifle Association did not give up the war. Biding its time, the organization was able to defeat attempts to renew the assault weapons ban. When the act expired in September 2004, members of the public could again legally own military-type rifles.

Gun Rights Groups and Law Enforcement Clash

Diana Lambert

The National Rifle Association (NRA) historically has had a close relationship with law enforcement. Local police forces often teamed up with the organization to offer gun safety classes to the public and to train police officers in marksmanship. Starting in the 1970s, however, the NRA's increasingly hard line against gun control legislation, led to a conflict with law enforcement organizations.

In the following selection, Diana Lambert, a political science professor at John Cabot University in Rome, describes the increasing tension between law enforcement and the NRA. Lambert deals in particular with law enforcement's attempts to ban armor-piercing "cop-killer" bullets, to pass the Gun Owners Protection Act (1986), and to outlaw guns that can evade detection by security equipment. In all these efforts, law enforcement lobby groups such as the International Association of Chiefs of Police (IACP) found themselves in head-to-head battles with the NRA. Law enforcement lobbying helped the gun control cause so much that Sarah Brady, the nation's best-known antigun campaigner, said that the Brady Bill could not have passed without law enforcement's help.

Diana Lambert began her academic career after serving nearly twenty years as a legislative analyst for the National Aeronautics and Space Administration (NASA).

One of the most important changes in the universe of interest groups involved in the gun control debate has been the growing support of police organizations for gun control.

Diana Lambert, "Trying to Stop the Craziness of This Business: Gun Control Groups," in *The Changing Politics of Gun Control*. Lanham, MD: Rowman & Littlefield, 1998, pp. 174–79. Copyright © 1998 by Rowman & Littlefield Publishers, Inc. All rights reserved. Reproduced by permission.

Historically, the police and the NRA have enjoyed a close, mutually supportive relationship. Since its founding in the late nineteenth century, the NRA has taught gun safety to generations of hunters and provided the training to scores of policemen on the beat. Internal changes in the NRA, beginning with the so-called Cincinnati Revolt of 1977,[1] undermined the cordial police-NRA relationship and transformed the NRA into a national lobbying powerhouse with a reduced emphasis on gun safety, hunting, and training into a group whose raison d'être is the rigid opposition to any law or regulation that placed any controls on the ownership, possession, or transportation of firearms. The NRA's strident defense of the unregulated, individual "right to bear arms" ultimately resulted in a schism with the police; law enforcement parted company with the NRA after many years of cordial relations and tentatively crossed the line into gun control territory.

The Struggle over "Cop-Killer" Bullets

The first crack in the NRA-police alliance came with the legislative struggle over the "cop-killer" bullet. Representative Mario Biaggi, Democrat from New York and a 28-year police veteran who had been shot ten times in the line of duty, was asked by the New York Patrolman's Benevolent Association to sponsor legislation to ban armor-piercing bullets. KTW bullets, or "apple greens" for the green coating of Teflon on the tip, were developed in 1970, ironically by a medical coroner and several police friends; it seems that the police were increasingly frustrated in the pursuit of suspected criminals who were able to get away by simply jumping in a car, totally unperturbed by the fusillade of police bullets that pinged off the car's metal frame. Law enforcement wanted a bullet that could penetrate an automobile; it got the apple green. But this powerful bullet turned out to be very dangerous: it went in one side of a car and out the other, creating havoc. In short order,

1. At the 1977 meeting of the National Rifle Association, a cadre of hard-line members took over leadership.

state legislatures banned these ballistics, but that did not stop a 1981 *NBC News* segment on "cop-killer" bullets or the ensuing congressional melee over federal legislation to ban these ballistics.

Michael Beard, director of the National Coalition to Ban Handguns, which later became the Coalition to Stop Gun Violence, contacted the NRA in an effort to reach a mutual agreement to ban these bullets; however, the gun lobby, fresh from its purifying Cincinnati Revolt, was in no mood for compromise: it would oppose a ban on armor-piercing bullets. Police organizations supported the bill, however, and after the NRA discovered that its opposition to the legislation was causing serious erosion of its relationship with the police, its lobbyists worked with the Reagan White House to draft a compromise administration bill. In June 1984, Ronald Reagan presented the police with a fait accompli—legislation that banned several but not all armor-piercing bullets. A less than comprehensive bill banning certain specific ammunition, including some types of cop-killer bullets, was ultimately signed in August 1985, its legislative journey in the new Congress hardly noticeable. The NRA was looking ahead to a much more significant legislative struggle, and the gun lobby wanted police help.

The McClure-Volkmer Act

But NRA-police relations were further eroded by the struggle over the McClure-Volkmer Act in 1986, which weakened the Gun Control Act of 1968. The Firearms Owners' Protection Act, (S 49 and HR 945), sponsored by Senator James McClure (R-ID) and Representative Harold Volkmer (R-MO), was intended to eviscerate the regulations put into place by the modest Gun Control Act of 1968 on the selling, ownership, and possession of all firearms, including handguns. The police, still very much legislative novices, again faced off with the NRA. In fall 1985, as law enforcement officers stood at attention in the Capitol, the Senate passed the McClure-Volkmer Bill. The police have undergone a road-to-Damascus experience[2]: "It was at that point that we realized we had to organize in some fashion, to be able to present ourselves as a large organized group to the legislators—to offset the tremendous lobbying capability of the NRA."

Police Oppose Repeal of Gun Control

So police groups began to organize to support gun control. Perhaps the single most critical step the police took was the October 1985 establishment of an umbrella group to coordinate their legislative efforts: the Law Enforcement Steering Committee Against S. 49. The steering committee also provided political cover for the many police officers and chiefs of police around the country who wished to voice their personal support for gun control, something that had been in the past professionally dangerous. Police associational magazines began to churn out editorials expressing clear opposition to McClure-Volkmer: "There's absolutely no good reason to relax the gun laws already on the books. If anything, they should be strengthened . . . S. 49 and HR 945 are irresponsible and reprehensible pieces of legislation" [stated an editorial in *Police Chief* magazine]. These same journals also engaged in grassroots lobbying, printing appeals to law enforcement officers to contact their members and senators to express opposition to the legislation. A letter signed by ten police organizations was sent to President Reagan, calling on him to oppose McClure-Volkmer. Then disagreement between law enforcement and its erstwhile allies became ugly and personal: an NRA chapter tried to revoke the NRA membership of the president of the International Association of Chiefs of Police (IACP), John J. Norton, citing his support for gun control legislation and his appearance before a House subcommittee that was critical of the McClure Volkmer legislation. This incident prompted a

2. This refers to the New Testament story of the conversion of Saul (later called Paul) while on the road to Damascus (Acts 9:1-8).

quick rebuttal in the form of a public letter from the IACP to the NRA and served to magnify the increasing estrangement between the two groups. . . .

Despite the direct and indirect lobbying activities on the part of the police organizations, the House passed the McClure-Volkmer Bill. [Criminologist William Poerner recalled:] "The police were on hand in full force. More than 100 blue-uniformed officers, representing major law enforcement associations, formed an accusatory gauntlet outside the House of Representatives as Congressmen filed in to consider [the bill]. Later, after checking their own arms, the police filled two sections of the spectators' gallery to watch the debate." The House, under the steady gaze of the police, nevertheless passed the bill, but with an amendment to retain the provision of the Gun Control Act of 1968 that banned the interstate sale of handguns. The Senate subsequently approved the House version, and the McClure-Volkmer Bill became law on May 19, 1986. The Law Enforcement Steering Committee was successful several months later in nursing through Congress a modest modification to McClure-Volkmer to address several very specific police problems; for example, firearms transported across state lines may not be stored in the glove compartment of an automobile. After its failure to stop the McClure-Volkmer Bill, the steering committee was not disbanded but retained with a new mandate: to address possible future legislative problems for the police. Hence the police had achieved a permanent and potentially sophisticated lobbying capability.

Police and NRA Split over Plastic Guns

The McClure-Volkmer legislation was a significant defeat for law enforcement and other gun control advocates, and it was also the beginning of a critical and long-term rift between the police and the NRA. The split widened during the debate over plastic handguns. The issue of plastic guns arose after the Department of Defense concluded from a commissioned study that disposable machine guns were not possible; gun control advocates got wind that the manufacturers were planning to use that study to examine the feasibility of plastic handguns and alerted the media. In a 1986 series of reports, syndicated columnist Jack Anderson alerted the public to the existence of something called the Glock 17, a foreign plastic gun that allegedly could pass through airport security stations undetected. The Reagan administration was actually ready to propose a bill to ban plastic guns when the NRA in behind-the-scenes negotiations convinced Attorney General Edwin Meese to shelve the bill. [Author Osha Davidson wrote,] "While police groups were growing adept at playing the image game—dubbing armor-piercing bullets 'cop killers' and framing other issues they cared about as either being pro- or anti-law enforcement—they were still no match for the NRA at back room lobbying. The police simply weren't as well connected as the NRA, which now had a decade of experience playing the game of power politics." With the administration effectively muzzled, the gun control groups convinced Senator Howard Metzenbaum in fall 1987 to introduce a bill to ban plastic guns. Predictably, the NRA announced its opposition, arguing that the guns could not evade airport security (the evidence was not conclusive) and that any gun control represented an opening in the floodgates that would result in the ultimate banning and confiscation of all firearms, including long guns. The NRA mobilized its enormous grassroots lobbying operation; Senate leaders delayed floor consideration until 1988. Much like in the cop-killer-bullet scenario, the White House worked out a draft bill with the NRA that banned some plastic and ceramic guns and offered the proposal to the police as a take-it-or-leave-it proposition. The Undetectable Weapons Act was signed into law November 11, 1988, but the debate had widened the split between the NRA and law enforcement.

Police Ally with Gun Control Groups

Police groups proceeded with their efforts to create a grass-roots lobbying campaign, exhorting their members to contact the Congress: [Police Chief C. Roland Vaugh claimed,] "Still we do not have effective federal legislation that protects our citizens from the dangers posed by handguns." The International Association of Chiefs of Police in 1988 went on record in support of a waiting period for handgun purchases, and by so doing, the law enforcement establishment entered for the first time into a compact with Handgun Control, Inc., (HCI) to seek the enactment of the Brady Bill.[3] Although it is clear that HCI has helped the police organize into a lobbying force, law enforcement is reticent about this new relationship; after all, there is a long history of alliance with the NRA. HCI heartily embraced this coalition with law enforcement. Upon the enactment of the Brady Bill, in an advertisement in *Police Chief* magazine (January 1994), Sarah Brady professed to the police, "We have finally done it and I do mean WE! Without the strong support of the International Association of Chiefs of Police and the individual police chiefs across the country, the Brady Bill would not be the Brady Law." The coalition was acknowledged at the White House signing ceremony for the Brady Bill, where Jim and Sarah Brady and IACP president Sylvester Daughtry were in attendance.

With the police endorsing a ban on the sale and manufacturing of assault weapons, [noted later IACP president John T. Whetsel,] the IACP "launched a blitz to convince the 75 undecided lawmakers to vote" for the assault ban legislation pending before the House, commenced a prodigious grassroots campaign to convince local police officers to speak out to Congress, and sent its president to testify before congressional committee. Subsequently, the assault weapons ban became law in 1994; this issue made the law enforcement–NRA estrangement, which had started out as a repairable fissure in 1985, a permanent chasm.

3. The Brady Bill was eventually passed into law and required a waiting period and background check for gun purchases.

From Civil Liberties to Crime Control

Police officials are now regular witnesses at committee hearings and are called for counsel by both congressional parties and the White House. The police, which prior to 1986 had allowed others to carry their water and had been betrayed by them, now are demanding a seat at the table of public policy, and the policy they seek is gun control. Gun control is now a law enforcement issue; gun control is now a crime issue.

The shift of police organizations from allies of the NRA to supporters of gun control has helped transform the debate on gun control from one centering on individual liberties (the right to bear arms) to one of crime control. It has also helped to erase the image that support for gun control comes only from liberals. The potential for police organizations to mobilize public support for gun control initiatives is clear. Yet it was not inevitable that the police would become part of the gun control coalition—the changed tactics of the NRA are largely responsible.

The Brady Bill Is the Centerpiece of American Gun Control

James B. Jacobs

The Brady Bill, passed in 1993, is the main national gun control law in the United States. Building on the 1968 Gun Control Act, it requires gun dealers to obtain the results of a background check on prospective gun purchasers. Prior to Brady, those seeking to buy a gun simply had to swear they had no criminal record, history of drug abuse, or mental illness that would disqualify them from owning a gun. Initially, under Brady the background checks were to be carried out by local or state officials. This requirement of the Brady Law was found unconstitutional, but by 1998 a federal database, the National Instant Criminal Background Check System (NICS), allowed weapons merchants to check on their prospective customers instantly.

In this selection, James B. Jacobs, a law professor at New York University and author of Can Gun Control Work? *and* Busting the Mob: United States v. Cosa Nostra, *explains how the Brady system developed. According to Jacobs, the most lasting impact of the law may be that it forced states and the federal government to update systems of recording and accessing criminal records.*

Like practically all gun control debates, the Brady Bill debate swirled around symbols and slogans. People tended to declare themselves for or against gun control, in principle. Those "for" gun control favored passage of the Brady Bill. Those opposed to gun control, of course, viewed the Brady Bill unfavorably. Even among partisans with strong views, probably few could explain what the Brady Bill actually said.

James B. Jacobs, *Can Gun Control Work?* New York: Oxford University Press, 2002, pp. 77–97. All rights reserved. Copyright © 2002 by Oxford University Press. Used by permission of Oxford University Press.

The Brady Bill Builds on Earlier Legislation

The Brady Law built on the regulatory scheme established by the 1938 Federal Firearms Act (FFA) and extended by the 1968 Gun Control Act (GCA). The GCA required that before selling a firearm, a Federal Firearms Licensee (FFL) [a federally licensed gun dealer] had to obtain from the purchaser a signed "Statement of Intent to Purchase a Firearm" (Form 5300.35). The purchaser had to swear that he or she did not have a criminal record, was not a drug abuser, and didn't fall into any other disqualifying category. The FFL had to verify the purchaser's in-state residency and age. A purchaser who knowingly provided an FFL with false information about eligibility was guilty of a federal crime punishable by a $10,000 fine, a maximum of 10 years' imprisonment, or both. The GCA also made it a federal felony for a person who had ever been convicted of a felony to possess a firearm; it also made it a felony for any person (whether or not an FFL) to knowingly transfer a firearm to a person with a felony record.

The GCA's regulatory scheme had at least two major defects, only the first of which was addressed by the Brady Law. (1) There was no check on the truthfulness of the firearm purchaser's affirmation of eligibility; thus, if the purchaser was willing to lie about his felony record, he could instantly obtain a firearm. (2) The GCA's regulatory scheme only applied to sales by FFLs; an ineligible purchaser could, without filling out any forms, buy a firearm at a gun show or from a private person who was not an FFL.

The Brady Law mandated that after November 30, 1998, the background checking system would be fully automated, so that FFLs could obtain an immediate authorization to complete a gun sale. The system in place prior to the implementation of the automated background checking system is referred to as "interim Brady"; the system after December 1, 1998, is referred to as "permanent Brady."

Finally, the Brady Law applied only to those states ("the Brady States") that did not already have a waiting period of at least five days or a handgun licensing or permitting requirement. The new law had no effect on how guns were sold in 18 states which already had laws at least as strict as Brady.

Interim Brady (1993–1998)

The law's major impact in the "Brady states" was the requirement that FFLs notify the chief law enforcement officer (CLEO) in the dealer's jurisdiction of a pending firearm sale. The law instructs the CLEO to make a "reasonable effort" to determine that the prospective purchaser is not ineligible under federal law to purchase a firearm. The FFL had to hold off transferring the firearm to the would-be purchaser until the CLEO approved the sale, or until five business days passed without a response from the CLEO, whichever occurred first. In effect, this meant a limited (up to five business days) waiting period for a firearm purchase. FFLs who knowingly failed to comply with Brady faced up to one year in prison, a fine, or both. Congress mandated that BATF [Bureau of Alcohol, Tobacco and Firearms] provide FFLs with training on Brady Law compliance, and it authorized BATF audits to assure that FFLs understood the process and maintained proper records. There was no punishment or penalty for a CLEO who failed to fulfill the background checking responsibility. Moreover, the Brady Law provided CLEOs with immunity from civil liability arising from "failure to prevent the sale or transfer of a handgun to a person whose receipt or possession of the handgun is unlawful . . . or for preventing such a sale or transfer to a person who may lawfully receive or possess a handgun." . . .

The Brady background check was based on a name check, not on fingerprints or social security number. The CLEO would conduct a name search in criminal records databases to determine whether the purchaser had a criminal record. If the CLEO did not match the prospective purchaser's name to any felony conviction, indictment, misdemeanor domestic violence conviction, or civil restraining orders, he could not block the sale. If the CLEO did not notify the FFL within five business days that the sale was blocked, the FFL could complete the sale. In the event that a rejected purchaser asked for a written explanation, the CLEO had 20 business days to provide it. A still-dissatisfied purchaser could appeal to a designated state agency.

If the sale was approved, the law required the CLEO to destroy the paperwork on the purchase, thereby preventing the formation of a government database on gun owners, that is, a national firearms registry. The FFL, however, was required to retain copies of the BATF form for 20 years and produce it for the police in the event of an investigation tracing the ownership of a firearm believed to have been used in the commission of a crime. (An FFL who goes out of business must turn over his records to the BATF.) The BATF conducts random inspections of FFLs (limited by law to once per year) to audit compliance.

Upgrading State Criminal Records

The Brady Law set November 30, 1998, as the deadline for the National Instant Criminal Background Check System (NICS) to be up and running. At the time that Brady became law, many states' criminal records systems were nowhere near ready to support a computerized background check system. In addition to being incomplete, the records did not contain information on the final disposition of a large percentage of arrests. The records in many states were not computerized. In other states, records were incomplete due to lengthy delays in entering cases into computer databases. In 1993, many observers did not believe that it would be possible within five years to upgrade state criminal records so that they would be available for automated on-line searching. Some gun control proponents believed that the idea of a computerized instant check system, originally offered by Republicans as an alternative to Brady, was a stalling tactic by the NRA and its congressional allies. The attorney general acknowledged that such a database could not be created "overnight," but only with "significant efforts and expenditures on the part of both the states and FBI."

The U.S. Department of Justice (DOJ) spearheaded an effort to upgrade the quality of state criminal history records. The Bureau of Justice Statistics (BJS) launched the Criminal History Records Improvement (CHRI) program in order to improve the completeness, accuracy, and timeliness of state criminal records. . . .

The Brady Act required the [U.S.] attorney general to develop computer hardware and software for "linking state record collections into a nationwide system that would enable instant responses to inquiries." Each state was required to have 80% of its criminal records available to the national system within five years after Brady's enactment. The attorney general issued timetables for each state. . . .

The Brady Amendments

The Brady Law was amended twice, between 1994 and 1998, to add to the categories of persons ineligible to purchase firearms. Both additions resulted from successful lobbying by women's groups, not gun control lobbyists. The Violence against Women Act (VAWA), part of the 1994 Violent Crime Control and Law Enforcement Act, was an omnibus effort to protect women from male violence. The law's best-known provision (which the U.S. Supreme Court held unconstitutional) provided female victims of domestic (and other male-sponsored) violence a right to sue their attacker for monetary damages in federal court. For our purposes, the law is important because it made ineligible for firearm ownership persons convicted of a "domestic violence misdemeanor" and persons subject to a court order restraining them from harassing, stalking, or threatening an intimate partner. VAWA also authorized technical assistance and training programs to assist states in entering data on domestic violence and stalking into the local, state, and national criminal record databases.

The strongest opposition to VAWA's gun control provision came from police organizations that had strongly supported the 1993 Brady Act. They objected that, due to domestic violence convictions, some police officers would lose the right to carry firearms and therefore their capacity to function as full-fledged law enforcement officers. In *Fraternal Order of Police v. United States*, the D.C. Court of Appeals upheld this firearms disqualification.

VAWA placed new and more challenging demands on state records systems, which are far less accurate for misdemeanors than for felonies. It therefore prompted a new round of efforts to improve state criminal records. But there remains a real problem in determining what counts as a domestic violence misdemeanor. In most states, domestic violence assault is not a specific statutory offense; men who abuse their wives and girlfriends are charged with assault or aggravated assault. Therefore, a criminal record would only indicate a misdemeanor assault conviction, not the gender of the victim, the perpetrator's motivation, or the relationship between offender and victim. Creating the kind of domestic assault database envisioned by VAWA would thus require substantive criminal law reform or a much more detailed criminal records system. Even then, there would be no easy way to know whether past assault convictions involved a domestic violence situation. . . .

Conclusion

The 1968 GCA made it a federal crime for an individual with a felony record (or certain other disqualifications) to possess a firearm. It also made it a crime for any person, including an FFL, knowingly to sell a firearm to a person with a felony criminal record. The GCA required a prospective handgun purchaser to sign a form attesting to his or her eligibility to own and possess a handgun. But the FFL had to take the purchaser's word for it.

The Brady Law provided for an independent check on the purchaser's eligibility. The Brady Act's background check requirement furthered the existing federal handgun regulatory regime's goal of preventing persons with criminal records from purchasing a handgun from FFLs by strengthening the GCA. Interim-Brady imposed a de facto waiting period (up to five days) on prospective handgun purchases. From 1993 to 1998, Interim Brady required the FFL to hold off on the sale (for up to five business days) until the CLEO had an opportunity to check the prospective handgun purchaser's criminal record. Permanent Brady requires that the FFL hold off on the sale of both long guns and handguns for up to three days, while the purchaser's name is run through either the FBI's NICS system or the state's POC [point of contact] system. If the search finds disqualifying information, the FFL is instructed not to make the sale.

In retrospect, the upgrading of state criminal records may prove to be the Brady Law's most lasting achievement. The states used federal grants to modernize their criminal justice records. State and federal criminal records databases have become far more comprehensive and accessible than they were in the early 1990s. This has implications for more informed law enforcement, pretrial detention and release decisions, charging, plea bargaining, and sentencing.

Waiting Periods and Background Checks Will Prevent Gun Crimes

Sarah Brady

The Gun Control Act of 1968 made it illegal for a convicted criminal, drug abuser, or person with a history of serious mental illness to purchase a gun. However, nobody checked a potential gun buyer's record to ensure compliance with this law. A gun buyer simply had to swear that he or she was not disqualified from owning a weapon. In most states, a purchaser could pay for the gun and take it home immediately.

The Brady Bill included a proposal to institute a waiting period of up to five days on handgun purchases. During the waiting period, firearms retailers were to give information on the prospective purchaser to local law enforcement, who in turn would conduct a background check on the individual. If any criminal convictions or other disqualifying information turned up, the individual would not be allowed to purchase a gun.

In the following excerpt, Sarah Brady testifies to Congress on the need for this legislation. After her husband James was seriously wounded and permanently disabled during the assassination attempt on President Ronald Reagan in 1981, Brady took up the cause of gun control, becoming the nation's foremost campaigner for stricter gun control legislation. The Brady Bill was enacted into law by Congress in 1993.

Thank you for the opportunity to testify once again before this distinguished Subcommittee. My name is Sarah Brady. I am Vice-Chair of Handgun Control, Inc., a national citizens

Sarah Brady, "Statement of Sarah Brady," testimony before the House Subcommittee on the Constitution of the Committee on the Judiciary, March 8, 1988, in *Guns in America: A Reader*, edited by Jan E. Dizard, Robert Merrill Muth, and Stephen P. Andrews Jr. University Press, 1999. Reproduced by permission of the author.

organization working to keep handguns out of the wrong hands. I am here today in strong support of H.R. 975, introduced by Representative Edward Feighan. . . . This legislation establishes a seven-day waiting period and allows for a background check on handgun purchasers.

Having previously testified before this Subcommittee, I know many of you are familiar with my personal experience and my involvement with this issue. It seems odd to me that it is in question whether we should act to keep handguns out of the wrong hands. For that is what this debate is about—whether we allow convicted felons to simply walk into gun stores and immediately walk out with handguns.

A Tool to Enforce Existing Law

We already have a federal law prohibiting convicted felons, minors, people who have been adjudicated mentally ill, illegal aliens, and drug addicts from acquiring handguns. But what does that mean if we do not have the tools to enforce that law? And so I ask you today, do you believe that a convicted felon should be able to walk into a gun store and get a handgun instantly? I cannot believe that anyone could sanction that. Yet as long as we do not have a reasonable waiting period and give police the opportunity to run background checks, a convicted felon will have our seal of approval. That is why I am here today. I am making a very personal appeal to you because I believe you have a responsibility to act to keep handguns out of the hands which would misuse them. Handguns in the wrong hands result in tragedy. I do not say that theoretically. I speak from experience.

I know that you are familiar with what happened on March 30, 1981. At 2:30 P.M. that day, my husband, Jim Brady, was shot through the head by a deranged young man [John Hinckley]. Jim nearly died. The President nearly died, and two of his security men were seriously wounded.

It has been almost seven years now. March 30th [1988] marks the anniversary of the shooting. I often think about the other handgun tragedies which have taken place in these seven years that could have been prevented if there were a national waiting period. We must not wait another seven years for other tragedies to occur. We must not wait any longer. We need a national waiting period now.

John Hinckley's handguns were confiscated in October 1980 as he tried to board an airplane in Tennessee, where he was stalking President Jimmy Carter. Hinckley, a drifter, then gunless, needed to replenish his arsenal. In possession of a Texas driver's license and knowing that Texas had no waiting period or background check, Hinckley made the trip to Dallas to purchase the handgun he used to shoot my husband and the President of the United States. Hinckley no longer lived at the address he listed on the federal form he was required to complete. A simple check might have stopped him. Had police been given an opportunity to discover that Hinckley lied on the federal form, Hinckley might well have been in jail instead of on his way to Washington. Now Jim lives daily with the consequence of Hinckley's easy access to a handgun.

This bill does not change who is legally permitted to purchase a handgun. Nor does it impose a major burden on law-abiding citizens. This legislation also provides that if an individual has a legitimate, immediate need for a handgun, the waiting period can be waived by local law enforcement. Is seven days too much to ask a responsible citizen to wait when we know that so many lives are at stake? I don't think so.

A Waiting Period Has Wide Public Support

Public support for a waiting period and background check is strong. A 1981 Gallup Poll found that more than 90 percent of Americans want such a law. This legislation is supported by every major law enforcement organization in the nation, many representatives of which are here today to testify in support of this bill. The American Bar Association, the American Medical Association, the AFL-CIO [American Federation of Labor-Congress of Industrial Organizations] and other organizations too numerous to mention, all support a federal seven-day waiting period. The 1981 Reagan Administration Task Force on Violent Crime recommended such a law. A 1985 Justice Department report states that "at minimum, the acquisition of a firearm by a felon should be somewhat more complicated than just walking into a gun shop and buying one."

While the National Rifle Association [NRA] opposes this bill, it is important to note that several years ago in its own publication, the NRA stated that a waiting period would be effective as a means of "reducing crimes of passion and in preventing people with criminal records or dangerous mental illness from acquiring guns."

The NRA has flip-flopped on waiting periods and recently taken extreme positions on machine guns, cop-killer bullets, and plastic guns. Considering these extreme positions, I find it incomprehensible that any Member of Congress could trust the judgment of the NRA on a national waiting period or any legislation affecting American lives and public safety, especially when the NRA is in direct opposition to America's law enforcement community which is charged with the responsibility of protecting us.

The NRA argues that proscribed persons do not purchase their handguns over the counter and certainly will not do so if they have to submit to a waiting period. Yet, a 1985 Department of Justice study entitled "The Armed Criminal in America" found that over 20 percent of criminals obtain their handguns through gun dealers. In fact, in states with waiting period laws, many criminals and others disqualified from buying handguns have been caught trying to purchase their handguns over the counter. Law enforcement officials from across the nation report tremendous success where waiting periods are in effect.

Screening Gun Purchasers Prevents Crime

For example, according to a police official in Memphis, Tennessee, the state's fifteen-day waiting period screens out about fifty applicants a month, most of whom have criminal records.

According to the California Department of Justice, the state's fifteen-day waiting period screened out more than 1,500 prohibited handgun purchasers in 1986. In that same year, Maryland's seven-day waiting period caught more than 700 prohibited handgun buyers.

States with waiting periods have been effective in stopping criminals before tragedy occurs, but it is unfortunate that in states without waiting periods or background checks, police do not have the same tools to prevent such tragedy.

One of the most shocking and disturbing cases of 1987 occurred in Florida in the wake of the October stock market crash. Arthur Kane purchased a handgun only forty-five minutes before murdering his Florida stockbroker and wounding another. If police had been able to conduct a background check, they could have discovered that Kane was a convicted felon.

In another well-publicized event, Dwain Wallace, who had a history of mental illness, was able to instantly purchase a handgun from a Youngstown, Ohio pawnshop. Just two days later, he brandished the handgun in the Pentagon and was immediately gunned down by a Pentagon guard.

A convicted felon, Larry Dale, purchased a handgun at a Tulsa, Oklahoma gun shop, and within twenty-four hours opened fire at a grocery store, killing one customer and wounding another.

I have described a few of the many well-known cases of proscribed persons who instantly purchased their handguns over the counter without having to undergo a waiting period or background check. But for each well-known case, there are many, many more which never make the front page.

While I am not suggesting that a waiting period will stop all crime, it is obvious from these examples that we can save many lives if we want to.

The NRA claims that waiting periods do not prevent criminals from obtaining handguns because criminals will get them from other sources. But in reality, it is the states without waiting periods that are a significant source of handguns for criminals.

The Treasury's Bureau of Alcohol, Tobacco and Firearms' study of handguns used in crime found that of all the handguns used in crime in New York City, only 4 percent were purchased in New York State, which requires a background check. Virtually all the rest were from states without waiting periods or background checks. In addition, the study found that in states without waiting periods or background checks, an overwhelming majority of handguns used in crime were purchased within the same state. For example, of all the handguns used in crime in Dallas, almost 90 percent were purchased in Texas, which has no waiting period.

A Nationwide Law Is Needed

The NRA argues that waiting periods should be left up to the states, not the federal government. While individual states, many counties and municipalities have passed local waiting periods, a national law is critical because it will ensure that handguns are not purchased over the counter in states without waiting periods and then sold on the street in states requiring waiting periods and/or background checks.

I am ashamed that my own state of Virginia, which has no waiting period or background check, is a major source of handguns used in crime elsewhere. Just a few weeks ago, police arrested one Richmond man who reportedly purchased more than seventy guns in Virginia and then brought them into Washington, D.C., to sell on the street. Another man from the District [of Columbia] was charged with using false identification, purchasing more than two dozen semi-automatic handguns in Virginia and selling them to District drug dealers. Unfortunately, these examples represent only the tip of the iceberg of this criminal traffic in handguns.

We can prevent needless tragedy. We can make it more difficult for criminals to get handguns. I hope that the day will come when no American family has to go through what my family has suffered. Again I ask, do you really believe that a convicted felon should be able to walk into a gun store and instantly purchase a handgun? The American people do not believe that. But until action is taken on this bill, a convicted felon purchasing a handgun will have our seal of approval.

The NRA would like to turn back the clock to the days before passage of the 1968 Gun Control Act, which has served our nation well for nearly two decades. . . .

I ask that you stand with our law enforcement community and provide the leadership that will save lives by keeping handguns out of the wrong hands.

Waiting Periods for Gun Purchases Are Ineffective and Unconstitutional

David B. Kopel

David B. Kopel was a district attorney in Manhattan. He currently works for the Independence Institute, a libertarian think tank, where he specializes in gun rights issues.

In testimony from 1988 before a U.S. Senate subcommittee, Kopel speaks against an early version of the Brady Bill. He sees the proposed law's waiting period and mandatory background check for handgun purchasers as an unacceptable violation of Second Amendment rights. Kopel first questions the proposed law's effectiveness. Contrary to claims by gun control advocates, he argues, the law will have no effect on crime. More specifically, he challenges the belief that a waiting period and background check would have led police to arrest John Hinckley before the 1981 attempted assassination of President Ronald Reagan, in which Reagan press secretary James Brady was wounded and disabled.

Citizens should not have to wait for police permission to exercise their Constitutional rights. Reporters who wish to file stories, even about national security matters, should not be required to pre-clear them with government officials. Women who choose to exercise their right to abortion should not have to submit to a waiting period. Citizens who wish to protect themselves should not have to wait to receive police permission.

Some people wonder why anyone would object to a seven-day waiting period. Seven days is too long for a woman whose

David B. Kopel, "Testimony on the Brady Amendment," U.S. Senate Subcommittee on the Constitution of the Committee on the Judiciary, August 2, 1988. Reproduced by permission.

ex-boyfriend is threatening to come over and batter her. Seven days is too long for families when a burglar strikes three homes in a neighborhood in one week, and may strike that night. Moreover, the imposition of a waiting period changes the Constitutional right to bear arms into a mere police-granted privilege.

A National Waiting Period Would Not Reduce Gun Crime

Every single study of waiting periods has found them to be absolutely useless in stopping gun crime. Professor Matthew DeZee states, "I firmly believe that more restrictive legislation is necessary to reduce the volume of gun crime." Yet his study of waiting-period laws showed them to have not the slightest effect. Professors Joseph P. Magaddino and Marshall H. Medoff, both of California State University, Long Beach, came to exactly the same conclusion. Another anti-gun scholar, Duke University's Philip Cook explains: "Ineligible people are less likely to submit to the screening process than are eligible people . . . because these people find ways of circumventing the screening system entirely." Cook concludes: "[T]here has been no convincing proof that a police check on handgun buyers reduces violent crime rates." When the Senate Judiciary Committee investigated the issue, the Committee found no evidence that waiting periods affect crime.

Waiting periods have existed in some states for over half a century. Yet after all this time, there is not a single criminological study ever published which shows waiting periods to have any beneficial impact.

The unanimous studies by the criminologists comport with common sense. Said Willis Ross, a former police chief, and currently lobbyist for the Florida Police Chiefs Association: "I think any working policeman will tell you that the crooks already have guns. If a criminal fills out an application and sends in his application . . . he's the biggest, dumbest crook I've ever seen."

As a National Institute of Justice study concluded, felons get guns on the street, or from friends, or they steal them. They do not walk into stores, and fill out background check forms.

A Waiting Period Would Not Have Stopped Assassination Attempt

Mrs. Sarah Brady, the nation's most prominent anti-gun lobbyist, claims that if the waiting period had been in effect, John Hinckley would not have shot her husband and President Reagan. As part of the national media campaign in favor of the waiting period, she asserts that Hinckley "lied on his purchase application. Given time, the police could have caught the lie and put him in jail."

That Mrs. Brady and HCI [Handgun Control, Inc.] use such a demonstrably false anecdote shows how weak their case really is. When asked for identification by the gun dealer, Hinckley offered his valid Texas driver's license. The address on the license was Hinckley's last valid address, a rooming house in Lubbock. (At the time of the gun purchase, he had no permanent address.) For the police to find the so-called "lie" would have required them to send an officer to check Hinckley's listed address, and determine that he no longer lived there. Since many police departments do not have the time to visit the scene of residential burglaries, it is rather absurd to expect them to have the time to visit the home of every single prospective handgun buyer.

Moreover, under the Brady amendment, the police would not be verifying Hinckley's address as reported on the federal multiple handgun purchase form. They would only be conducting a background check, and would have found that Hinckley had no criminal or publicly available record or mental illness.

Drug Dealers Will Not Be Stopped

Another inaccuracy in the campaign for a national waiting period is the claim that it will help disarm drug dealers. It is simply preposterous to imagine that any kind of gun legislation, including a waiting period, would have the slightest impact on drug dealers.

Drug dealers obviously cannot count on the police or the courts for protection from violence. Because of this, and because they are a valuable robbery target, it would virtually be suicide for them not to carry a gun.

In addition, drug dealers cannot use normal legal and social commercial dispute resolution mechanisms. Like the gangsters of alcohol prohibition days, drug dealers need guns to protect their business's income and territory. Thus, many drug dealers must own a gun for their lives and their livelihood.

No matter how scarce guns become for civilians, there will always be one for a criminal who can pay enough. Street handguns now sell for less than $100. If the price went up to $2,000, dealers would still buy them, because dealers would have to. Spending a few hours' or days' profits on self-protection is the only logical decision for a dealer. Can anyone really believe that an individual who buys pure heroin by the ounce, who transacts in the highly illegal chemicals used to produce amphetamine, or who sells cocaine on the toughest street-corners in the worst neighborhoods will not know where to buy an illegal gun?

Police Testimony

Several high-ranking police officials, purporting to represent the nation's police, have stated that a waiting period would be beneficial. That testimony is highly dubious.

First of all, it is simply untrue that these police bureaucrats represent the sentiment of the nations's police. In 1987, the Florida Legislature repealed a host of local waiting periods, and that repeal took place thanks to the lobbying of the

Florida Police Chiefs Association. In a national survey of all the nation's chiefs of police and sheriffs, 59% percent said that a national seven-day waiting period would not be helpful.

More fundamentally, the opinion of police chiefs is not the arbiter of our Constitutional rights. Some police executives criticize the exclusionary rule; they claim that a strong fourth amendment causes crime. Some police executives criticize the grand jury system, and claim that a strong fifth amendment causes crime. Some criticize the Miranda decision, and claim that a strong sixth amendment causes crime. The police executives here today say that a strong second amendment causes crime. In every case the executives are wrong.

In fact, the actual effect of this legislation will be to decrease crime-fighting resources, and thereby increase crime. There are at least six million handgun transfers per year. How many hours would it take for a policeman to run a national criminal records check, and to visit the home of every person who applied?

One hour, at the very least. That would be six million police hours spent checking up on honest citizens, instead of looking for criminals. In the haystack of applications by honest citizens, police will search for a few needles left by the nation's very stupidest criminals. Looking for crime, police officers will be directed into a paperwork enterprise particularly unlikely to lead to criminals. Wouldn't all those millions of police hours be better spent on patrol; on the streets instead of behind a desk?

Gun Registration Increases Police Power

The asseverations of some police officials that waiting periods have helped them stop large numbers of criminal handgun purchases ought to be taken with a grain of salt. The fact that police officials may deny a handgun permit does not prove that the applicant was a criminal—more likely, that official was capriciously denying a citizen his Constitutional rights. . . .

In short, the fact that some police officials reflexively oppose the exercise of Constitutional rights is not entitled to much weight in the deliberative process. Congress has repeatedly rejected their unreasoned arguments, and should do so again. (By the way, actual police officers—as opposed to officials who specialize in lobbying—strongly support Second Amendment rights.)

Another reason that some police chiefs favor this proposal is that police chiefs, like any other administrators of large government offices, often seek to expand their official power. From the perspective of a police administrator (who may never even have served in street patrol) more power means more officers doing administrative tasks. It is the same mentality that leads to the creation of paperwork empires in the Pentagon or in the Hubert H. Humphrey Building [which houses the Dept. of Health and Human Services], even if the emphasis on paperwork hinders the agency's performance of its assigned mission.

Turning the right to bear arms into a police-granted privilege is one flaw of the bill, and its criminogenic effects are another. These problems are obvious enough, but there are more problems revealed when one examines the bill's particulars.

De Facto Gun Registration

First of all, the bill claims to be just about waiting periods, but it turns out to include de facto gun registration. Applicants must submit not only to identification for a background check, but also "an accurate description of the handgun," and "the serial number of the handgun."

The police are theoretically supposed to destroy the statement of an applicant who is not denied permission to buy. Yet there is nothing in the bill to punish police who keep a photocopy or a computer entry. (Indeed, the bill only requires that the statement itself be destroyed, not the same information in another form.) Further, no one doing a background check on an applicant needs to know the gun's make or serial number. The only point of those items being required, therefore, must be for later use. Gun registration, incidentally, is itself quite useless in crime-fighting.

Onerous Paperwork Requirements

At a time when local police resources are already stretched thin, the bill imposes very substantial paperwork and manpower requirements on every police force in the country. The bill claims it is cost-free, because the background check will be optional. But the bill's prime lobbyist, Handgun Control Inc., has already announced that its legal defense fund will sue police departments that do not implement the background check. . . .

Police officers and gun dealers will not be the only people burdened by paperwork, for the bill applies even to private gun transfers. Suppose a father wishes to give one of his handguns to his daughter, who lives alone in a dangerous neighborhood where several rapes have occurred recently. The daughter must swear out a written statement, then the father must send the statement, along with photo identification of the daughter (and a description of the identification) in a certified or registered letter (return receipt requested) to the chief of police. After seven days, if the police have not vetoed the sale (and the daughter has not yet been raped or killed), she may receive the gun. The father must keep on file his own copy of the daughter's sworn statement for at least a year; if he fails to do so, he is subject to a $500 fine.

Paperwork like this does not uphold the law. Rather, it diminishes respect for the legal system, as citizens are niggled to death with self-evidently silly paperwork requirements.

When citizens deal with the government, the Fifth Amendment guarantees them due process of law. This is true for everything from public library cards to driver's licenses. It is all the more true when Constitutional rights are involved.

Yet the national waiting period bill provides no appeal from police decisions. If a police department denies applicants for specious reasons, or no reason at all, the applicants have no remedy. In Maryland, where an appeals process exists, the police are over-ruled 85% percent of the time, as previous testimony on this bill has revealed.

In this context, one should remember that some American police departments have a proven record of lawless enforcement of the gun laws. The St. Louis police have denied permits to homosexuals, nonvoters, and wives who lack their husband's permission. Although New Jersey law requires that the authorities act on gun license applications within 30 days, delays of 90 days are routine; some applications are delayed for years, for no valid reason. Mayor Richard Hatcher of Gary, Indiana, ordered his police department never to give anyone license application forms. The Police Department in New York City has refused to issue legally-required licenses, even when twice commanded by appeals courts to do so. The Department has also refused to even hand out blank application forms.

Federal Gun Laws Violate State's Rights

Finally, the national waiting period is offensive to the Tenth Amendment[1], and to principles of federalism. Most states, including Senator [Howard] Metzenbaum's state of Ohio, have rejected waiting period proposals. In the last 15 years not a single state has instituted a waiting period. Indeed, the trend has been against waiting periods, with Florida repealing its waiting periods, and other states enacting pre-emption laws to prevent localities from imposing such laws. There is no compelling federal need to over-ride the decisions of these states.

1. The Tenth Amendment reserves to the states all the powers not specifically granted to the federal government.

There is no federal need to impose mountains of paperwork on state and local police agencies. That is why President Reagan, who favors waiting periods at the state level, has announced his opposition to the national waiting period proposal.

The national waiting period bill will most likely be offered as an amendment to the drug bill, on the Senate floor. The claim that it would have the slightest effect on drug dealers is patently absurd. The claim that the bill would have prevented the assassination attempt on President Reagan is a falsehood. The only evidence for the proposal comes from government administrators who are reflexively hostile to individual rights. Their claims contradict all the academic evidence, and they contradict common sense. As a first step in the destruction of the right to bear arms, the national waiting period is splendid. It is not part of the war on drugs; it is part of the war on the Constitution.

CHAPTER 5

Gun Control Issues
and Activism

Chapter Preface

The terrorist attacks on America on September 11, 2001, changed the political landscape in the United States. Suddenly, combating terrorism became the top priority—and nearly the only priority—for Congress, the president, and the nation. Gun control dropped from the political agenda. As a way of regaining political momentum, gun control advocates have sought to link the issue of gun violence with terrorism. In publicity materials and reports, gun control advocacy groups highlight how terrorists bypass security checks by purchasing weapons at gun shows. On the other side, gun rights groups promote an image of armed American citizens defending themselves against terrorists.

One of the leading proponents of gun control in the United States Senate is Frank Lautenberg of New Jersey. He has pointed out that the federal government seems unconcerned that terrorists can easily procure firearms. "As our government confiscates toenail scissors at airports, secures power plants, and increases domestic surveillance . . . we're ignoring the most obvious threat that's out there, and that is the ease [with] which terrorists can access weapons in virtually any town across the country." Lautenberg has proposed requiring that information from criminal background checks be kept longer and cross-checked against government terrorist watch lists. He received some support from a March 2006 Government Accounting Office report stating that thirty-six individuals on these terrorism watch lists had been able to purchase firearms in 2005.

Gun rights advocates are concerned that Lautenberg's proposals go too far in interfering with a citizen's right to bear arms. They believe that Americans are safer if they have the means to defend themselves against terrorism. Gun advocates often point to the example of Israel, where many citizens carry weapons due to the constant threat of terrorism. Jon Dougherty of the gun rights group Gun Owners of America notes that in February 2002, "a Palestinian terrorist was attempting to set off an explosive device in yet another crowded Israeli market, when an 'alert shopper' recognized what he was doing and shot him dead." Wayne La Pierre of the National Rifle Association advocates arming airline pilots in order to defend against hijackings. Rather than having to rely on government, say gun control opponents, citizens should be trusted to protect themselves.

People on both sides of the gun control issue have seized on the terrorism issue in order to advance their cause. No doubt the controversy over terrorism and gun control will continue, as have those surrounding other issues in the gun control debate.

Terrorists May Obtain Weapons at Gun Shows

Loren Berger and Dennis Henigan

Dennis Henigan is the legal director of the Brady Center, a pro-gun control organization. Loren Berger is a researcher and investigator based in Washington, D.C. In the following excerpts from the Brady Center's report "Guns and Terror," Berger and Henigan describe several examples of how terrorists use legal loopholes to obtain weapons. Gun shows are a particularly easy way for terrorists to get handguns, rifles, and even grenade launchers. Berger and Henigan contend that the lack of background checks for sales at gun shows, coupled with varying state regulations, makes the United States a veritable weapons supermarket for terrorists around the world. Groups as different as the Islamic militant group Hezbollah and the Irish Republican Army have used gun shows to supply their arsenals. Berger and Henigan call for action on the part of Congress to regulate sales at these shows.

The ATF [Bureau of Alcohol, Tobacco and Firearms] estimates that there are more than 4,000 gun shows annually, convened in every region of the country. The ATF's own gun trafficking investigations "paint a disturbing picture of gun shows as a venue for criminal activity and a source of firearms used in crime." A review of its gun trafficking investigations conducted during the period July 1996 through December 1998 revealed that gun shows were "a major trafficking channel" and were associated with the diversion of approximately 26,000 firearms into the illegal market.

Loren Berger and Dennis Henigan, "Guns and Terror," Brady Center to Prevent Gun Violence, 2001, pp. 5–11. Copyright © 2001 by Brady Center to Prevent Gun Violence. All rights reserved. Reproduced by permission.

Terrorists Shop at Gun Shows

Gun shows are a unique marketplace because they feature both federally licensed dealers and unlicensed sellers. In most states, however, background check requirements only apply to sales by licensed dealers; that is, persons required to obtain a federal firearms license because they are "engaged in the business" of selling guns. Indeed, background checks mandated by the Brady Act and many state laws have proven to be an invaluable tool to deny guns to terrorists. For example, in October [2001], the Anti-Terrorism Task Force in Portland, Oregon arrested Ali Khaled Steitiye, a convicted felon who claimed to have trained at Lebanese guerilla camps, after a background check stopped him from buying an assault rifle from a licensed dealer. At gun shows, however, there are thousands of gun sales without background checks by vendors claiming not to need a federal license because they are merely selling from their "personal collections" of guns. Thus, felons and other prohibited gun buyers can easily avoid criminal background checks by shopping at gun shows, where a diverse group of sellers are willing to do business with "no questions asked." Gun shows also are notorious venues for unscrupulous licensed dealers willing to make illegal sales. It is difficult to imagine a more inviting marketplace for terrorists and those who seek to supply them with lethal weaponry.

Still, Congress has failed to pass legislation to close the gun show loophole that allows unlicensed or "private" sellers to sell guns at gun shows without background checks. Although a gun show bill sponsored by Senator Frank Lautenberg (D-NJ) passed the Senate in 1999, it died in the House. In this [the 107th] Congress [2001–2002], bills to close the loophole have been introduced in the Senate by Senator Jack Reed (D-RI) and by Senator John McCain (R-Arizona) and in the House by Rep. Michael Castle (R-Del.).[1]

1. These bills failed to pass out of committee.

Gun Show Pipeline: From Michigan to Lebanon

On September 10, 2001—just one day before the devastating attacks on the Pentagon and the World Trade Center—Ali Boumelhem was convicted on a variety of weapons violations plus conspiracy to ship weapons to the terrorist organization Hezbollah in Lebanon. He and his brother Mohamed had purchased an arsenal of shotguns, hundreds of rounds of ammunition, flash suppressers and assault weapon parts from Michigan gun shows, according to press reports.

Had it not been for a police informant, they might have eluded any scrutiny. Neither federal nor state laws in Michigan require background checks between a private or unlicensed gun seller and a buyer. Mohamed had a clean record, but Ali was legally prohibited from purchasing firearms as a result of a felony grand-theft conviction.

Ali Boumelhem was arrested in Detroit in November of 2000 before he could depart on a one-way ticket back to Lebanon, along with Mohamed, who was also indicted on conspiracy charges, but acquitted. According to press reports, the arrests came after a lengthy surveillance and the discovery on a Lebanon-bound ship of an auto-parts container whose cargo included the firearms, ammunition and gun parts. Federal agents said they watched Ali, a resident of Detroit and Beirut, travel to gun shows to buy gun parts and ammunition for shipment overseas. An ATF and FBI informant also told investigators that he had seen Ali in Beirut with automatic weapons and explosives, as well as grenades and rocket launchers. . . .

Florida Gun Show Dealer Arms Irish Republican Army

To the young Irish Republican Army [IRA] soldier from Belfast in pursuit of firearms, south Florida was a gun fanatic's free-for-all. "We don't have gun shows in Ireland, and you see things here like you never imagined," Conor Claxton said.

Within weeks of Claxton's arrival in the U.S. in the spring of 1999, he and three associates spent more than $18,000 on dozens of handguns, rifles and rounds of high-powered ammunition. They hid the arms inside toy firetrucks, computers and clothing, and then mailed their purchases overseas where they were intended to be used against the British government in Northern Ireland. Police intercepted 23 packages containing 122 guns and other weapons originating from the group.

Claxton enlisted three U.S. residents, all natives of Northern Ireland and the Republic of Ireland, to buy the weapons. The team obtained crucial assistance from a licensed firearms dealer—Edward Bluestein, the owner of Big Shot Firearms in Delray Beach, Florida. Bluestein sold at least 43 handguns to associates of Claxton, who also bought weapons from other collectors and private citizens, but Bluestein was the operatives' main source, and he agreed not to report all of the sales on required federal forms in exchange for an extra $50 per gun.

Gun dealer Bluestein was approached by IRA operatives Anthony Smyth and his girlfriend Siobhan Browne, a naturalized U.S. citizen, at a gun show at the National Guard Armory in Fort Lauderdale in April 1999. They wanted to buy quality handguns that could be easily concealed. Bluestein obliged them and invited them to his home. Browne reportedly told Bluestein the guns would be used for a cause she and Smyth were "deeply devoted to." The two also told Bluestein the guns would be shipped out of the country and the serial numbers on the firearms would be obliterated.

Bluestein admitted that he received warnings from his fellow gun dealers at the armory, who were particularly suspicious of the intense interest of a woman, Siobhan Browne, in amassing numerous guns. "Other sellers there said, 'Be careful of her,' but I thought what a bunch of old ladies," Bluestein said. "Lots of people collect handguns. I had some of the lowest prices there. That's why she came to me."

In all, Smyth and Browne negotiated with Bluestein to buy more than 100 weapons. In just a few weeks time, and before law enforcement authorities caught on to the scheme, 43 firearms had changed hands—Israeli pistols, Austrian semi-automatics, Smith & Wesson revolvers, and others. Bluestein courted even more business from the group, although he suspected the guns could wind up in the hands of assassins. Bluestein testified he had put up thousands of dollars of his own money to fill one of the team member's demands, and when that customer left him holding an order of 18 guns, Bluestein contacted him again to try to keep the shady deal alive. "I was totally trapped, what could I do? ... I'm sitting there in debt from a transaction that's supposed to make me a rich man," Bluestein said in blunt defense.

On July 6, 1999, British authorities noticed suspicious packages arriving with cargo at West Midland International Airport in Coventry. The labels said they contained toys, computers and baby clothes, but when the packages were X-rayed, police saw the image of a Ruger .357 Magnum. The serial number that was supposed to have been rendered illegible traced to Bluestein and Big Shot Firearms. British and Irish police, Scotland Yard's anti-terrorist unit and the FBI's Joint Terrorism Force intercepted many more of Bluestein's firearms in packages mailed to Ireland in August 1999.

In September 2000, Claxton, an admitted officer of the IRA, was sentenced to approximately five years in federal prison for shipping the guns to Northern Ireland. The other collaborators each received shorter sentences for conspiring to carry out Claxton's mission.

Bluestein, who had agreed to cooperate with prosecutors, pleaded guilty to conspiring to export guns illegally. He received probation for two years, including six months of house arrest.

Domestic Terrorists Seek
a Grenade Launcher

Only a lack of money kept Charles Kiles and Kevin Patterson from buying a grenade launcher to blow up two huge liquid propane storage tanks in a suburban community outside of Sacramento, California. A gun show dealer, Ronald Rudloff, recently testified in federal court that he nearly sold the rocket-propelled weapon to the pair at a January 1999 gun show in Las Vegas.

Rudloff said that Kiles put on his glasses to inspect the grenade launcher. With Rudloff's permission, Kiles shouldered it and looked through the illuminated scope. Kiles then motioned for Patterson to join him and said, "Kevin, come on over and look at this. This is what we need," according to Rudloff. Rudloff then explained to Kiles the weapon could be made operable simply by removing a pin placed in it by federal authorities.

Kiles, 51, and Patterson, 44, revealed they were members of the San Joaquin County (California) Militia. The conversation turned to rumors of threats by militant groups to be timed with the end of the millennium. Rudloff recalled Kiles saying, "We're going to have a big bang ourselves. We're going to take out a couple of propane tanks."

Rudloff's grenade launcher was priced at $2,200. "They wanted to take it with them, but they couldn't come up with the funds," Rudloff said in court during an October 2001 criminal proceeding against Kiles and Patterson. The two men were being tried on charges of conspiring to build and use a "weapon of mass destruction" to destroy the tanks, located in the vicinity of both a residential and commercial development near Sacramento.

According to press reports, the militiamen called their targets—the two tanks holding 24 million gallons of liquid propane—the "twin sisters." Their goal, federal investigators said, was to create such chaos on or around the New Year that the president would declare martial law—giving militant groups an opportunity to overthrow the government.

The California militiamen—frequent visitors to gun shows—were discovered to have had more than 50 firearms and 50,000 rounds of ammunition between them when their homes were searched in connection with their scheme to blow up the propane tanks. Agents also seized a trove of bomb-making chemicals and about 30 pounds of fertilizer that could be turned into explosives.

Kiles had been able to obtain guns even though he was personally prohibited from owning them due to a previous violation of firearms laws. In 1992, he had pled guilty to felony possession of an assault rifle. In November 2001, a jury dead-locked 11-1 to convict Kiles and Patterson. They are currently awaiting a new trial.[1] . . .

Gun Shows Provide a Loophole

With the exception of a handful of states, there are no restrictions on the number of guns that can be purchased from retail gun dealers. Because there is no centralized, national record keeping of gun purchases, it is difficult for law enforcement even to determine whether someone has bought a large number of guns. This is of great help to terrorists and gun traffickers, who are interested in purchasing as many guns as possible as quickly as possible, without detection.

Federal law enforcement authorities have long known that the purchase of large numbers of guns—particularly handguns—by a single buyer is an indicator of gun trafficking into the illegal market. For this reason, there is a special provision in federal law that requires that purchases of two or more handguns within a five business-day period be reported by licensed gun dealers to the ATF. This reporting requirement,

1. Kiles and Patterson were found guilty of conspiracy to use a weapon of mass destruction and conspiracy to use a destructive device in a new trial in 2002.

however, is hardly a deterrent to trafficking. According to the ATF, handguns sold in multiple sales accounted for 22 percent of all handguns traced to crime in 1999.

In 1993, Virginia, weary of its reputation as the primary source state for crime guns trafficked to New York and other northeastern cities, enacted a landmark state statute curbing multiple sales. Virginia's statute limits purchasers to one handgun per month. The statute had a dramatic effect on gun trafficking from Virginia. For example, of the crime guns recovered in New York, the percentage traced back to Virginia fell by 61 percent. However, only three other states—South Carolina, Maryland and California—place any quantity limits on gun buys. Moreover, the gun industry has done nothing to voluntarily limit large-volume sales, an issue raised in the various liability lawsuits brought by municipalities against the industry. The absence of a uniform federal limit on large-volume sales ensures a robust illegal market that is the terrorists' best source of lethal weapons.

Gun Control Will Not Prevent Terrorism

Wayne LaPierre and James Jay Baker

Wayne LaPierre is the executive vice president and chief executive officer of the National Rifle Association. James Jay Baker is an attorney and lobbyist in Washington, D.C. He has been associated with the National Rifle Association as an attorney since 1980. In addition, he writes a monthly column for Shooting Times *magazine.*

In the aftermath of the 9/11 attacks, some gun control advocacy groups and pro-gun control politicians sought to highlight the connection between guns and terrorism. In this selection LaPierre and Baker argue against the linking of privately owned guns with terrorism. They point out that the al Qaeda hijackers used boxcutters, not guns, on September 11, 2001. They also challenge some misleading statements in pro-gun control groups' efforts to link the gun industry with terrorism. For example, they note that large-caliber rifles found in the possession of al Qaeda members were actually supplied by the United States government, not by private companies or individuals. LaPierre and Baker accuse politicians such as Senators John McCain, Ted Kennedy, and Charles Schumer of exploiting Americans' fear of terror in order to introduce more gun restrictions.

Smoke was still curling over the ruins of the World Trade Center when the gun-control lobby swung into action, seizing on that tragedy to score points in the political arena.

Seven days after the attack, the Brady Center to Prevent Gun Violence issued its first press release linking terrorism and the danger of guns in the home. About three months af-

Wayne LaPierre and James Jay Baker, *Shooting Straight: Telling the Truth about Guns in America*. Washington, DC: Regnery Publishing, Inc., 2002, pp. 10–13. Copyright © 2002 Henry Regnery Company. All rights reserved. Reproduced by special permission.

ter the attack, the Brady Center issued a report, "Guns and Terror: How Terrorists Exploit Our Weak Gun Laws." Despite the fact that all nineteen terrorists commandeered airplanes not with guns, but with boxcutters and other crude knives, the cover of the report was adorned with an evil-looking man in a typical Moslem outfit peering at the reader through the scope of a rifle. The report should have been named: "How the Gun-Control Lobby Exploits Tragedy to Terrorize Americans."

Less than a month after September 11, gun-control advocates at the Violence Policy Center chimed in, issuing a report called "Voting from the Rooftops: How the Gun Industry Armed Osama bin Laden, Other Foreign and Domestic Terrorists and Common Criminals with .50-Caliber Sniper Rifles."

After reading that, you might want to throw this book down, lock the door, and close the shutters (after looking up and down the street for a terrorist). What's this about? The Violence Policy Center is harping on the sale, *in the late 1980s*, of twenty-five high-powered, military-style sniper rifles that were provided to the Afghan resistance of the Soviet invasion *by action of the U.S. government*. You'll recall that during the Reagan administration, there was strong bipartisan support in Washington, D.C., for people who, at that time, were popularly known as "Afghan freedom-fighters." Yes, some of them later became terrorists and turned against the United States. That's hardly a news flash. Yet the Violence Policy Center treats this chapter of U.S. foreign policy as if it were a domestic gun issue.

Do you think that's an honest treatment of the issue? Do you think that's a very respectful way to deal with the memory of September 11?

Chris W. Cox, the new executive director of the NRA's [National Rifle Association's] Institute for Legislative Action, is a hunting buddy of the authors, and the point man for making our case on campaign finance reform and other critical issues. Many people who represent issues on Capitol Hill speak in a roundabout way. Chris doesn't mince words when it comes to the red herring of terrorism and gun shows.

"This lowers the level of debate," he says. "September 11 had nothing to do with lawful gun owners and lawful gun shows. This should be offensive to every American and every gun owner."

You might think that at least elected officials would be above exploiting tragedy in this way for political gain. You would be wrong.

Before 2001 was out, Senators Ted Kennedy [D-MA] and Chuck Schumer [D-NY] pushed a bill that would amount to national gun-buyer registration. They have long wanted the Department of Justice to retain the records of the National Instant Check System (NICS), the computerized system that exists solely to determine whether a person seeking to buy a gun has a criminal record. By retaining the records of the law-abiding citizens who clear the system, the Department of Justice would in effect create a national database with which to confiscate guns. (. . . [T]hat is not as far-fetched as it sounds. The recent history of other countries, including Canada, shows how registration quickly leads to confiscation.)

How did Kennedy and Schumer exploit September 11?

Their bill is now called the "Use NICS in Terrorism Investigations Act." But it's still the same old gun-control bill.

"Now we've got the terrorist issue," boasts Representative John Conyers of Michigan, in talking about his innocuous-sounding proposal for extending background checks that would effectively kill gun shows in America. "There are very few in the general population who are going to tolerate a loophole through which these weapons are allowed into the war to support terrorism. That is a no-brainer at this point."

All of these efforts pale in comparison to the sleek, sophisticated antigun campaign that goes by the winsome name of Americans for Gun Safety (AGS). On December 14, 2001, they put out a statement on the conviction of a Lebanese man named Ali Boumelhem for weapons charges.

The AGS statement drips with ominous speculation of a sort one used to read on the backs of dime-store novels.

It reads: "We don't know whether the Boumelhem case is part of a pattern or an isolated lone wolf. But we do know this—the agents of terror operating on our soil have navigated our freedoms to exploit airports, flight schools, colleges, financial institutions and libraries to strike at the heart of our country. Maybe they are not interested in using guns as part of their terror plans. Maybe they are interested only in dramatic attacks like bombs, planes, and the like. But the notion that they have not—or cannot—figure out that they can buy guns at gun shows with no questions asked is no longer credible."

The truth is, there are no laws or background checks that will keep a determined, sophisticated terrorist from getting his hands on a gun anywhere in the world, if that is what he wants to do. If the AGS reports are to be believed, this beloved American institution of gun shows—as old as the Republic, one cherished as much by gun collectors as auto buffs love auto shows, or devotees of earthenware love porcelain shows—has become a squalid bazaar of eye-patched, scar-faced international arms merchants who would scare the pants off Indiana Jones.

The AGS freely throws around charges about terrorist organizations like Hamas and Hezbollah flocking to American gun shows—but the real target is the ordinary, law-abiding American who wants to sell his or her late father's deer rifle.

We won't get into a point-by-point refutation of these charges here. . . . The point is that after losing on so many fronts, the antigun crowd is back in business, fueled by rumor-mongering and appeals to fear.

What makes AGS insidious is that it has explicitly broken with other antigun groups in accepting the constitutionality of gun ownership. Its Web site offers a sepia-toned, nostalgic picture of a hunter toting a shotgun. It strikes a reasonable pose, suggesting that it doesn't want to get rid of guns, just make sure that they are used safely.

What is going on here? The people behind AGS understand that they have lost time and again on efforts to move toward explicit, direct banning of the use of guns for personal safety. So they are seeking to enact laws that would make it harder for law-abiding people to own guns. They are doing this one waiting period, one restriction at a time. These are people who know when to give up on a frontal assault and try to flank the enemy.

What is AGS?

The most public faces of AGS are those of Senators John McCain and Joseph Lieberman.

It was McCain, you'll recall, who, backed by friendly big media, goaded his fellow senators until he passed what the media uncritically call campaign finance reform. Under this law, big media conglomerates like Viacom, the Disney Corporation, and General Electric have unlimited rights to spend money talking about issues and candidates (which, of course, is their constitutional right). These big, wealthy institutions own broadcasting companies and spend millions lobbying Congress, yet campaign finance reform leaves them alone. Left out in the cold are ordinary citizens and advocacy groups ranging from the National Rifle Association (NRA) to the American Civil Liberties Union, who would be forbidden by law from expressing their views in the weeks before an election. Under this new law, the NRA isn't even allowed to respond to charges by the broadcast media for weeks before an election. The punishment for violating this complicated law is prison sentences and stiff fines.

The intent of such a law is obvious. It is aimed at stifling the voices of gun-owning American citizens.

Better Regulation of Guns Will Save Lives

David Hemenway

In this selection, David Hemenway, a professor at the Harvard School of Public Health and the director of the Harvard Injury Control Center, argues that guns should be regulated just as other consumer products are. This regulation should have two aims: to keep guns out of the wrong hands and to make guns safer.

Comparing the United States with similar developed countries, such as Canada, Australia, and New Zealand, Hemenway finds that the other countries do a better job of preventing criminals from obtaining guns. He suggests that in the United States, laws limiting the number of guns purchased per month might cut down on gun running, thus keeping criminals from obtaining black market guns. He compares guns to automobiles, noting how government regulation and changes in automotive engineering have reduced fatality rates from traffic accidents. Hemenway believes that if the same level of regulation were applied to guns, gun fatalities would be drastically reduced.

In the United States, the rates of injury and death due to firearms and the rate of crimes committed with firearms are far higher than those in any other industrialized nation. Every hour, guns are used to kill four people and to commit 120 crimes in our country.

Comparison with Similar Societies

Perhaps the most appropriate international comparisons are among the United States and other developed "frontier" coun-

David Hemenway, "Regulation of Firearms," *New England Journal of Medicine*, September 17, 1998, pp. 842–45. Reproduced by permission.

tries where English is spoken: Canada, Australia, and New Zealand. These four nations have similar cultures, and all have histories that include the violent displacement of indigenous populations. They also have similar rates of property crime and violence. What distinguishes the United States is its high rate of lethal violence, most of which involves guns.

Gun-related deaths among children and adolescents are a particular problem in the United States. Among developed nations, three quarters of all murders of children under the age of 14 years occur in this country. More than half of children younger than 14 who commit suicide are Americans, even though the rate of suicide by methods other than firearms among children here is similar to that in other countries.

Canada, Australia, and New Zealand all have many guns (though not nearly as many handguns as does the United States). The key difference is that these countries do a much better job than we do of keeping guns out of the wrong hands. Their experience shows that when there are reasonable restrictions, relatively few outlaws can possess or use guns.

The Need for Stronger Safety Standards

Success in the United States in reducing motor vehicle injuries—we now have one of the lowest rates of death per vehicle-mile in the world—provides insight into methods that could reduce firearm injuries. In the 1950s, efforts to reduce motor vehicle injuries focused on the driver. Commonly presented statistical data seemed to show that almost all automobile crashes were caused by error on the driver's part. The greatest attention was thus paid to education and enforcement: training motorists to drive better and punishing them for committing safety violations. Despite these well-intentioned efforts, further success in reducing motor vehicle injuries had to await a more comprehensive approach.

165

Eventually, injury-control experts recognized that to increase the safety of driving, it would be more cost effective to try to change the vehicle and the highway environment than to try to change human behavior. People will always make mistakes, and sometimes they will behave recklessly. But when they do, should they die? Should others?

Thus, numerous alterations were made both in cars and in roads to make collisions less likely (better brakes, a third brake light, and divided highways, for example) and to make serious injuries more avoidable if there was a collision (collapsible steering columns, nonrupturable gas tanks, breakaway road signs, more advanced emergency medical systems, and so on). No one believes that today's drivers are more careful than those of the 1950s, yet the number of motor vehicle fatalities per mile has been reduced by more than 75 percent.

Firearms, like motor vehicles, lawn mowers, and chain saws, are consumer products that cause injury. The safety of virtually every consumer product is regulated by federal or state government. The conspicuous exception is the gun, which, per minute of exposure, is probably the most dangerous of all such products. Unfortunately, because firearms have been deliberately exempted from the oversight of the Consumer Product Safety Commission, we are in the indefensible position of having stronger consumer-protection standards for toy guns—and teddy bears—than for real guns.

Stronger safety standards can help make firearms less dangerous. At a restaurant during a recent American Public Health Association convention in Indianapolis, a patron bent over and a derringer fell from his pocket. The gun hit the ground, discharged, and wounded two convention delegates. This person had a permit to carry the gun, and the firearm met all relevant safety standards—of which there are none. Anecdotes such as this demonstrate why such standards are needed.

Public Support for Gun Regulation

Survey results reported in this issue of the *Journal* by Teret et al.[1] provide evidence that the majority of Americans want to see guns treated and regulated as consumer products. In nationally representative polls, at least two thirds of all respondents were in favor of six policies that would enhance the safety of new guns. Examples of these policies are childproofing, personalization (which prevents firing by an unauthorized person), and indicators that show whether the gun is loaded. These measures may not substantially reduce gun-related crime, but they are inexpensive and could decrease the number of deaths and injuries that occur each day as a result of unintentional gunshots.

In one state, Massachusetts, the attorney general, who is the state officer responsible for protecting consumers' rights, recently issued regulations implementing several of these moderate safety standards for firearms sold in the state. Domestic gun manufacturers and firearm-sports organizations are challenging his authority to ensure, among other things, that firearms are childproof and meet the safety standards required of imported guns. Both these measures are favored by more than 80 percent of gun owners and non–gun owners alike in the national sample polled. . . . We can expect that similar conflicts will develop in other states as new regulatory policies are invoked.

Keeping Guns Out of the Wrong Hands

These recent polls also show very high public support, among both gun owners and non–gun owners, for innovative policies designed to keep guns out of the wrong hands. One proposed type of law would prohibit the purchase of guns by persons who have been convicted of any one of various felonies, such

1. The survey results are in the article "Support for New Policies to Regulate Firearms: Results of Two National Surveys," *New England Journal of Medicine*, September 17, 1998, pp. 813–18.

as assault and battery. Another set of requirements would reduce illegal gun sales by, for example, state adoption of one-gun-per-month laws to decrease gun running across state lines. Such moderate measures would limit the easy access to guns by those most likely to misuse them, while imposing only a slight inconvenience on "decent, law-abiding citizens." Previous surveys have shown that most Americans, most gun owners, and even most self-reported members of the National Rifle Association are in favor of many moderate measures that could reduce gun injuries. Unfortunately, most of these measures have not been enacted.

The United States has more cars per capita than any other developed nation. Because of reasonable policies to regulate automobiles and roadways, we now have one of the lowest motor vehicle fatality rates. We are also a society with more guns per capita than any other developed nation. We can remain a nation with many guns yet control our gun-injury problem if we take reasonable steps to make firearms safer and to keep them out of the wrong hands. Few individual gun policies, if enacted alone, would substantially reduce the firearm-injury problem. Similarly, few individual highway-safety initiatives of the past 40 years, by themselves, made a great difference in reducing highway deaths. Together, however, many small policies can have a large effect. It is now quite clear that the implementation of policies focused exclusively on education and enforcement (training in the handling of guns and punishment for criminal violations) is not the most effective way to reduce our firearm-injury problem substantially.

Much can be done to decrease the gun problem in the United States without changing the fundamental availability of firearms for most citizens. In the past decade, the public health community has been studying this issue and has suggested many reasonable, feasible policies. Through such policies we can begin to change social norms, as we have with cigarette smoking and motor vehicle injuries. In the case of firearms, the norm to be changed is the one that accepts lethal violence as a part of everyday American life.

Policy Makers Lack Knowledge of America's Gun Culture

Philip Cohen and Andy Coghlan

Gun violence has a large impact on the United States. Gunshot wounds received in murders, suicides, and accidents cost almost thirty thousand Americans their lives in 2002. Yet despite the public health impact of guns, and years of debate over gun control, little is known about gun culture in the United States. A report by the United States National Academy of Sciences has argued that the lack of good data is hampering the ability to devise effective gun policy.

There are several reasons for the lack of quality data. Many studies have been poorly designed. For example, studies seeking to determine the effect of guns on suicide rates focus on rates of firearm ownership rather than whether guns were actually used in individual suicides. Another problem is that legitimate gun owners are often reluctant to answer questions about their use of guns while most criminals obviously do not answer surveys detailing their access to firearms.

Philip Cohen and Andy Coghlan are reporters for the popular British science magazine New Scientist.

Gun violence kills tens of thousands of people in the United States each year. Yet the basic characteristics of this modern social disease have never been studied in a rigorous way, according to a damning report by the US National Academy of Sciences (NAS).

It found that key intervention policies such as gun ownership laws and strategies for firearms education are based on poorly gathered or incomplete data and badly designed trials.

This means there are few established facts about the cause-and-effect relationship between guns and many types of violence, or the effectiveness of gun control or educational programmes intended to steer young people away from firearms. "While there is a large body of empirical research on firearms and violence, there is little consensus on even the basic facts about these important policy issues," the report says.

What is not in dispute is the impact of firearms on American society. The United States has the highest rate of firearms-related homicide in the industrialised world. In 2002, almost 30,000 Americans died from firearms injuries—suicide, homicide and unintentional shootings combined—about double the number of people who died from AIDS. Guns are the 12th most common cause of death overall, and second only to road vehicles in deaths caused by injury.

Little Known About Gun Culture

Yet very little is known about America's gun culture. "That's troubling because the conclusions we draw from any data out there are very important," says report author Robert Johnson, a paediatrician at the University of Medicine and Dentistry in New Jersey. "If we decide on a course of action, we better have the best possible evidence to back that up."

Concern about the state of firearms and violence research led the National Institute of Justice, Centers for Disease Control and Prevention and three private foundations to ask the NAS to study the issue. In choosing the panel, the academy deliberately included a number of experts who, like Johnson, had no experience in firearms or violence research but were experienced in designing rigorous scientific studies.

One of the strongest concerns voiced by the panel is that we still do not know who owns guns and how they use them. Criminals are unlikely to tell researchers about the illegal weapons they own, and legitimate gun owners are often reluctant to divulge details about their firearms. Researchers have come to accept that surveys of gun ownership and use will have a low response rate.

Better-Designed Studies Needed

This is where experience of other research areas can help, says Charles Wellford, a criminologist at the University of Maryland at College Park, who chaired the report panel. "In studies of illegal drug use or sexual assault, we've been able to dramatically improve response," he says. "The key was to recognise the problem and ask what can be done to solve it." Borrowing the successful "blind" technique from clinical trials or otherwise safeguarding the identity of participants is a strategy that needs to be explored for gun ownership, he says.

Another problem is that data on firearm use is not gathered in a way that is useful to policy makers. For example, in places where gun ownership is common, the rate of gun-related suicide is known to be high. But the poor design of studies examining the issue has prevented them showing whether guns increase the overall risk of suicide or whether their absence would simply drive anyone intent on suicide to choose another method. Flawed studies tend to look at rates of gun ownership and suicide, rather than individual details of each death and whether guns were involved.

Overall, says the report, there has been no systematic effort to gather information on gun use, partly because the task is so daunting.

A similar lack of research is also apparent in countries such as the United Kingdom where gun crime is climbing steadily. Gun-related offences almost doubled in England and Wales between 1998 and 2003, from 13,874 a year to 24,070. While these account for less than 0.2 per cent of all crime, the government is taking the problem seriously. "There has been a rise over the years and that is unacceptable. We are doing everything we can to stop it," a spokesman for the United Kingdom's Home Office says.

Earlier [in 2004], the Home Office launched a public consultation exercise to help inform its policies on gun crime, but the ministry does not specifically seek feedback on the quality of research carried out. A report on the criminal use of firearms published in May by the Inspectorate of Constabulary identified shortcomings in data collection and intelligence.

"Statistical data on firearms incidents and gun crime is incomplete," it said. There were discrepancies in the way gun crimes were defined and recorded in different police forces, the report found. "Taken together, these all contribute to an uncertain overall picture."

The Goal Is to Prevent Gun Violence

Ultimately, the goal is not merely to understand the details of gun violence, but to understand how to control or prevent it. This is why the dialogue on guns in the United States is usually dominated by issues of intervention, such as gun control legislation and education programmes. However, the report's authors found that what few studies have been done didn't determine whether either type of intervention cuts gun violence. And some experts worry that educating young people about the dangers of guns might actually enhance the allure of the weapons.

The effectiveness of many of these strategies needs to be tested in the most scientifically rigorous manner possible, with a randomised controlled trial, says Robert Boruch, a statistician and expert on trial design at the University of Pennsylvania in Philadelphia, and another of the report's authors. "The good news is that the interest in better-quality evidence is there at a national level," he says. "People are realising that without strong science, you are left with rhetoric, romance and assumption."

The Effort to Hold Gun Makers Liable for Gun-Related Crime

Greg Sargent

New York City has some of the toughest restrictions on gun purchases and ownership in the United States. Despite these laws, guns find their way into the hands of those who are disqualified from possessing them in the city. Suspecting that major firearms manufacturers such as Beretta and Glock were turning a blind eye to the illegal trade in guns, New York decided to sue the companies for the costs associated with gun violence in the city. In doing this, officials were following the lead of New Orleans and other cities. However, other municipalities have not been successful in their legal efforts against gun makers; courts have been reluctant to blame any manufacturer for the illegal use of its product.

Despite the long odds, New York has pressed ahead with the lawsuit. The court case has attracted the attention of gun rights supporters in Congress, who have passed legislation aimed at protecting gun makers from liability. In addition, Congress passed a law to prevent the 'trace data'—information on the sale of guns from dealers to the public—from being released to those seeking to sue gun makers, making the lawsuit much more difficult.

Greg Sargent is a contributing editor at New York *magazine. He writes frequently for other left-leaning publications such as the* Nation *and the* American Prospect.

In 2004 [the law firm of Thelen, Reid & Priest teamed up] . . . with New York Mayor Michael Bloomberg to wage a landmark lawsuit against more than three dozen gun manu-

Greg Sargent, "The Ricochet," *Mother Jones*, vol. 30, September/October 2005. Copyright 2005 Foundation for National Progress. Reproduced by permission.

facturers and distributors. The companies—including Beretta, Smith & Wesson, Glock, and Browning—constitute virtually the entire firearms industry. New York City's case is built on the theory that gun companies know their products end up being trafficked to criminals and could take easy steps to stop it, but fail to do so. Thelen has been working pro bono on the case for a year, donating seven lawyers to the effort full time, and even putting its vice chairman, Michael Elkin, in charge of the case.

When a jury starts hearing *New York v. Beretta* this Fall [2005] in Brooklyn Federal Court, it will be the first time such a lawsuit brought by a municipality has made it to trial. A victory would be such a significant feat that GOP members of Congress, in a move some observers think is aimed at this lawsuit, are pushing for sweeping liability protection for the industry. Nonetheless, gun-control advocates see in the New York case a real possibility to force manufacturers to change the way they market and distribute their products. Even a partial victory could embolden other jurisdictions to bring cases and erode the industry's clout, just as early successes cracked Big Tobacco.[1]

New York Awash in Guns Despite Laws

It's a paradox that has frustrated law enforcement agents for decades: New York City has some of the strictest gun laws in the country—you can't buy a firearm if you don't have a license, are under 21, a felon, or have a mental disorder—yet thousands of such off-limits customers wind up with weapons, and the overwhelming majority of guns used to commit crimes were originally sold in perfect compliance with the law.

The explanation, experts say, is that traffickers import guns to New York, where the tight laws and, at least in certain areas, high demand drive up the price of illegal firearms. Traf-

---

1. The author refers to successful lawsuits that held tobacco companies liable for damage to smokers' health.

fickers know they can reap huge profits buying guns in the South, where prices are low and look-the-other-way dealers proliferate. *New York v. Beretta* alleges that the industry is well aware of the middlemen—gun shows, kitchen-table dealers, straw purchasers, and buyers who purchase in obviously excessive quantities—through which traffickers get the guns bound for the city's black market.

However traffickers procure them, many guns ultimately used in New York crime travel along I-95, a highway that New York cops have dubbed the "Iron Pipeline." Running from Florida up the East Coast, "it exemplifies the big problem New York faces," says Joe Vince, a 28-year veteran of the Bureau of Alcohol, Tobacco, Firearms and Explosives (ATF) and an expert witness for the plaintiffs. "In Ohio, for instance, the majority of guns come from in-state. But in New York, people are loading up on guns hundreds of miles from the city. How can the cops police that? It's ATF who has jurisdiction over interstate trafficking, but ATF only has 2,000 agents for 50 states. So very few traffickers are ever caught or prosecuted."

City Officials Begin Suing Gun Manufacturers

By the late '90s, gun-control advocates and municipal officials across the country started examining how corrupt dealers who feed such black markets get their goods. They found that the vast majority of gun dealers are law abiding, meaning that the payoff from zeroing in on the dirty ones could be disproportionately great. According to one widely cited study published by the [President Bill] Clinton administration in 2000, just 1.2 percent of dealers accounted for more than 57 percent of the guns used in crimes nationwide. If gun companies stopped their products from getting into the hands of such dealers, far fewer guns would flow into the local black markets—leading, it's hoped, to a commensurate drop in violent crime.

Beginning with New Orleans in 1998, a number of municipalities struck out in a bold new direction, suing gun manufacturers and distributors to recoup the medical and law enforcement costs of gun violence. Many built their cases around "trace data" compiled by the ATF. When a gun is used in a crime and recovered, the ATF retraces the path of the weapon from manufacturer up through any transactions conducted by licensed dealers. This information is not publicly available, but manufacturers have had access to it, which could enable them, adversaries say, to gauge which dealers are selling guns eventually used in crimes. They could be monitoring problem dealers and even cutting them off, but so far, few of them appear to have done so. That failure, some of the lawsuits have charged, amounts to callous, even willful negligence—the result of a reluctance to cut into profits made off of corrupt dealers. By this calculus, the actions of the industry lead to a grimmer conclusion: that gun companies actually help to create a black market. An analysis of ATF data performed by the National Economic Research Association found that 11 percent of guns sold in 1996 had been used in a violent crime by 2000. "It's become obvious that the crime gun market has been a huge segment of the gun industry's sales," says Brian Siebel, a senior attorney at the Brady Center to Prevent Gun Violence. "It's been a share of the market they haven't been willing to surrender."

Industry spokespeople insist that manufacturers aren't trained in law enforcement and are "no more responsible for criminal misuse of their product than Budweiser is responsible for drunk driving," in the words of Lawrence Keane, general counsel of the National Shooting Sports Foundation (NSSF), a well-funded industry group. What's more, gun companies have "done more than any other industry" to prevent bad sales and promote safety, says John Renzulli, a lawyer representing Glock and Browning, citing a program to educate dealers about straw purchases.

History of New York's Lawsuit

[Former New York mayor] Rudolph Giuliani launched New York's lawsuit in 2000. He'd just dropped out of the New York Senate race and, no longer beholden to the NRA [National Rifle Association] or national Republicans for financial contributions, he was more concerned with burnishing his legacy of battling crime. To that end, the suit was perfect. The legal term of art for the large-scale injury and death that resulted from [the] industry's lack of self-policing was decidedly understated: the gun companies were creating a "public nuisance." The city's top lawyer (known as the corporation counsel) explained in a press conference that "our major claim would be that the gun industry is guilty of negligent marketing and distribution." He vowed to recoup "tens of millions of dollars and maybe more."

Despite the big promises, little at the time indicated that New York had much chance of winning. A number of municipalities had brought similar cases, but none had succeeded in getting to trial. Individual victims of gun violence had won scattered cash settlements here and there, but they hadn't achieved anything approaching industry reform, and most had used different theories of liability. The year before, the NAACP [National Association for the Advancement of Colored People] had a public-nuisance suit on behalf of its members—in effect, potential victims of gun violence—trying to force a change in the industry's marketing practices, but that effort was not yet far along.

Indeed, the gun companies seemed confident that legal precedent was on their side. "Time after time, the courts have held that a manufacturer of a safe, nondefective product is not responsible for its criminal use," said Bob Delfay, then-president of the NSSF, when the New York suit was filed. "We're hoping Giuliani will regain his sanity by morning."

Delfay was cocky, but then again, the suit was far from a slam dunk. New York City had to make a different kind of argument from plaintiffs in traditional liability suits, in which manufacturers are held responsible for defective products, rather than ones that work all too well. Judges have shown resistance to cases that smack of regulating an industry through the courts. Gun companies had latched on to an argument that, without documented proof to the contrary, seemed plausible—namely, that their guns were sold and resold so many times en route to the streets that they couldn't know for sure which dealers were corrupt.

To counter this argument, the NAACP had subpoenaed the ATF trace data from 1995 to 1999. The industry found an ally in the ATF, which refused to comply with the subpoena. But the courts were another matter: In 2002 Judge Jack Weinstein, who heard the NAACP case in Brooklyn Federal Court, directed the ATF to turn over the information.

Saying that the NAACP couldn't show that its members had suffered a different kind of harm from industry practices than other New Yorkers, Weinstein subsequently dismissed the group's case, meaning that the ATF trace data would, for the time being, remain privileged. Nonetheless, Weinstein's decision appeared to set a precedent for future plaintiffs that such records could be pried loose. More important, he was sympathetic to the public-nuisance argument, writing in his opinion of the industry's "failure to take elementary steps" that "would have saved the lives of many people." Indeed, he found that while the industry had improved its practices in recent years, "these steps are late, too few and even now insufficiently embraced by most individual defendants to eliminate or even appreciably reduce the public nuisance they individually and collectively have created." . . .

Congress Steps In

Congress is currently considering a far-reaching bill—sponsored by Rep. Cliff Steams (R-Fla.) and Senator Larry Craig (R-Idaho), who's a board member of the NRA—that would grant the entire firearms industry immunity from a broad swath of liability lawsuits. Similar legislation passed the House in 2003 but was rejected by the Senate. . . . That, of course, was a different Senate, and at press time the bill's passage seems likely,[2] though what impact it could have on *New York v. Beretta* remains up in the air. Both sides say they expect to go to trial, suggesting that Weinstein could declare the law unconstitutional or find that it doesn't apply retroactively. "Judge Weinstein is a very creative guy," says NSSF counsel Keane. "He will find a way to make sure this case goes to trial."

Meanwhile, pretrial skirmishing, especially around the critical trace data evidence, has been heated. New York tried to get its hands on even more data than the NAACP had wrested from the ATF before its case died. But industry—backed by government allies—struck back repeatedly. In 2004, Rep. Todd Tiahrt (R-Kan.) even inserted a provision into an appropriations bill barring the use of subpoena power over ATF trace data. The agency dragged its feet on coughing up the information until June of 2004, when Weinstein ruled that the data had to be released to plaintiffs' lawyers.

The prospect of exposing such records at trial is already a victory, say gun-control advocates. "Not only will it identify the worst gun dealers in America, but it will also show beyond any doubt that the gun industry is profiting from sales to criminals carried out through those very same dealers," says the Brady Center's Brian Siebel.

Still, the city's legal hurdles are considerable. As there's no precedent linking industry sales practices to a public nuisance, "the first challenge is to show that the defendants owe the plaintiffs a legal duty, not just a moral or ethical one," says Ralph Stein, a professor at Pace University School of Law who's followed the case. Ironically, another disadvantage that the city faces is the perception that New York City is now very safe, compounded by the fact that some in the jury—the ju-

---

2. The bill passed in July 2005.

risdiction includes suburban (and fairly conservative) areas like Nassau and Suffolk counties—may be well insulated from violent crime. "We may not be able to say that the average commuter is feeling the nuisance," concedes [Thelen attorney Gabriel] Nugent, who won't get into too many strategic details about the trial. Another potential weak spot in the city's suit is that it doesn't center on the sort of tragic plaintiff juries respond to. "It has to bring home to the jury that the city's action, if successful, would protect all New Yorkers, starting with these 12 people," says Stein. . . .

As he prepares to launch what may be the most significant case in the history of gun litigation, Michael Elkin is confident of both short- and long-term victory. "These manufacturers have escaped responsibility for far too long," he says. "Their day of reckoning is coming."

Chronology

1689

The English Bill of Rights establishes a limited right to bear arms.

1791

The American Bill of Rights is ratified, including the Second Amendment to the Constitution: "A well regulated Militia, being necessary to the security of a free State, the right of the people to keep and bear Arms shall not be infringed."

1792

Congress passes the Militia Act, setting out federal guidelines for the training and equipping of state militias.

1813

Kentucky becomes the first state to pass gun control legislation.

1837

Arkansas and Georgia pass concealed-weapons laws.

1871

The National Rifle Association is founded.

1886

In *Presser v. Illinois*, the U.S. Supreme Court upholds the right of states to ban private armed militias.

1919

The War Revenue Act places a 10 percent excise tax on weapons purchases.

1927

Congress outlaws sending handguns by mail.

1934

Congress passes the National Firearms Act, which limits the possession and transport of some weapons such as submachine guns.

1938

Congress passes the Federal Firearms Act, which requires anyone selling firearms to obtain a license. Gun dealers must record names and addresses of weapons purchasers.

1939

In *United States v. Miller*, the U.S. Supreme Court upholds federal control on gun possession and transport.

1968

Congress passes the Gun Control Act, which outlaws mail-order sales of rifles and shotguns and bars convicted felons, drug users, and the mentally incompetent from purchasing guns.

1974

The National Council to Control Handguns is founded. (Its name is later changed to Handgun Control, Inc., then to Brady Campaign to Prevent Gun Violence).

1977

In the "Cincinnati Revolt," hard-liners led by Harlon Carter take control of the National Rifle Association.

1986

Congress passes the Law Enforcement Officers Protection Act, banning so-called cop-killer bullets, which can penetrate bulletproof vests.

Congress passes the Firearm Owners Protection Act, which eases restrictions on gun sellers while increasing punishments for various gun-related crimes.

1993

Congress passes the Brady Handgun Violence Prevention Act, which imposes a five-day waiting period and background check before gun purchases.

Congress passes the Violent Crime Control and Law Enforcement Act, which contains a ban on assault weapons.

1994

Congress passes legislation banning assault weapons.

1998

The Brady law goes into full effect with the activation of the National Instant Criminal Background Check System.

2004

The Assault Weapons Ban, passed in 1994, expires. It is not renewed by Congress.

Organizations to Contact

American Civil Liberties Union (ACLU)
125 Broad St., 18th Fl., New York, NY   10004-2400
(212) 549-2500
e-mail: aclu@aclu.org
Web site: www.aclu.org

The ACLU is a national organization that works to defend Americans' civil rights as guaranteed by the U.S. Constitution. The ACLU interprets the Second Amendment as a guarantee for states to form militias, not as a guarantee of the individual right to own and bear firearms. Consequently, the organization believes that gun control is constitutional and necessary. The ACLU publishes the semiannual *Civil Liberties* newsletter in addition to policy statements and reports.

The Brady Campaign to Prevent Gun Violence
1225 I St. NW, Suite 1100, Washington, DC   20005
(202) 898-0792 • fax: (202) 371-9615
Web site: www.bradycampaign.org

The Brady Campaign is the largest national organization dedicated to promoting gun control. The campaign seeks not to ban all guns, but to pass what it considers sensible legislation that will lead to a reduction in gun violence. It publishes the periodic *Brady Report Online Newsletter* as well as special reports such as *Smoking Guns: Exposing the Gun Industry's Complicity in the Illegal Gun Market* and *On Target: The Impact of the 1994 Federal Assault Weapons Act.*

Bureau of Alcohol, Tobacco, Firearms and Explosives
650 Massachusetts Ave., NW, Rm. 8290
Washington, DC   20226
(202) 648-8010 • fax: (202) 648-8001

e-mail: ATFMail@atf.gov
Web site: www.atf.treas.gov

The Bureau of Alcohol, Tobacco, Firearms, and Explosives is in charge of enforcing the nation's gun control laws. In its law enforcement capacity, ATF falls under the Department of Justice. The organization is responsible for granting federal licenses to firearms dealers. It is the primary agency charged with investigating firearms trafficking within the United States.

Citizens Committee for the Right to Keep and Bear Arms (CCRKBA)
12500 NE Tenth Pl., Bellevue, WA 98005
(800) 486-6963 • fax: (425) 451-3959
e-mail: informationrequest@ccrkba.org
Web site: www.ccrkba.org

CCRKBA promotes the view that the U.S. Constitution's Second Amendment guarantees and protects the right of individual Americans to own guns. The organization works to educate the public concerning this right and to lobby legislators to prevent the passage of gun control laws. The committee is affiliated with the Second Amendment Foundation. It publishes the books *Gun Laws of America, Gun Rights Fact Book, Origin of the Second Amendment*, and *Point Blank: Guns and Violence in America.*

Coalition to Stop Gun Violence
1023 Fifteenth St. NW, Suite 301, Washington, DC 20005
(202) 408-0061 • fax: (202) 530-0331
Web site: www.csgv.org

Formerly called the National Coalition to Ban Handguns, the coalition lobbies at the local, state, and federal levels to ban the sale of handguns and assault weapons to individuals. It also litigates cases against firearms makers. Its publications include various informational sheets on gun violence, *Stop Gun Violence Newsletter*, and *Firearms Litigation Reporter.*

Gun Owners of America
8001 Forbes Pl., Suite 102, Springfield, VA   22151
(703) 321-8585 • fax: (703) 321-8408
e-mail: goamail@gunowners.org
Web site: www.gunowners.org

Gunowners of America is an organization that opposes gun control legislation. It is even more hard-line than the National Rifle Association. Concentrating mostly on electronic media, the group offers a daily news summary of gun-related stories and e-mail alerts of interest to gun owners.

Independence Institute
13952 Denver West Pkwy., Suite 400, Golden, CO   80401
(303) 279-6536 • fax: (303) 279-4176
e-mail: Anne@i2i.org
Web site: www.i2i.org

The Independence Institute is a pro–free market think tank that supports gun ownership as a civil liberty and a constitutional right. Its publications include books and booklets opposing gun control, such as *Children and Guns: Sensible Solutions, The Assault Weapon Panic: "Political Correctness" Takes Aim at the Constitution*, and *The Samurai, the Mountie, and the Cowboy*.

Jews for the Preservation of Firearms Ownership (JPFO)
PO Box 270143, Hartford, WI   53027
(414) 673-9745 • fax: (414) 673-9746
e-mail: jpfo@jpfo.org
Web site: www.jpfo.org

JPFO is an educational organization that promotes the view that Jewish law mandates self-defense. Its primary goal is the elimination of the belief that gun control is a socially useful public policy in any country. JPFO publishes the quarterly *Firearms Sentinel*, the comic book *"Gun Control" Kills Kids!*, and the books *Gun Control: Gateway to Tyranny* and *Lethal Laws*.

Million Mom March
1225 I Street, NW, Suite 1100, Washington, DC   20005
(888) 989-MOMS • fax: (202) 408-1851
Web site: www.millionmommarch.org

The Million Mom March organization is a national network of mothers and others concerned about gun violence and its effect on children. The group was started to stage an actual march on Washington, D.C., that took place on May 14, 2000. The organization continues as a separate entity under the umbrella of the Brady Campaign to Prevent Gun Violence.

National Crime Prevention Council (NCPC)
1000 Connecticut Ave. NW, 13th Fl., Washington, DC   20036
(202) 466-6272 • fax: (202) 296-1356
e-mail: webmaster@ncpc.org
Web site: www.ncpc.org

The NCPC is a branch of the U.S. Department of Justice that works to teach Americans how to reduce crime. It provides readers with information on gun control and gun violence. The NCPC's publications include the newsletter *Catalyst*, published ten times a year; the book *Reducing Gun Violence: What Communities Can Do*; and the booklet *Making Children, Families, and Communities Safer from Violence*.

National Firearms Association (NFA)
PO Box 52183, Edmonton   T6G 2T5
   Canada
(780) 439-1394 • fax: (780) 439-4091
e-mail: info@nfa.ca
Web site: www.nfa.ca

The NFA in the primary reservoir of legal and legislative expertise in the Canadian firearms community. It provides research data, expert witnesses, and education to the firearms community and others. NFA publishes the monthly newsletter *Pointblank* as well as *Canadian Hunting and Shooting, Bowhunting*, and *Angler* magazines.

National Institute of Justice (NIJ)
PO Box 6000, Rockville, MD   20849
(800) 851-3420 • fax: (301) 519-5212
Web site: www.ncjrs.org

A component of the Office of Justice Programs of the U.S. Department of Justice, the NIJ supports research on crime, criminal behavior, and crime prevention. The National Criminal Justice Reference Service acts as a clearinghouse that provides information and research about criminal justice. Its publications include the research briefs "Reducing Youth Gun Violence: An Overview of Programs and Initiatives," "Impacts of the 1994 Assault Weapons Ban," and "Homicide in Eight U.S. Cities: Trends, Context, and Policy Implications."

National Rifle Association (NRA)
11250 Waples Mill Rd., Fairfax, VA   22030
(703) 267-1000
e-mail: webmaster@nrahq.org
Web site: www.nra.org

The National Rifle Association is not only the most powerful anti–gun control lobby, it is regularly voted one of the most powerful lobbies in the United States. Originally founded to promote marksmanship through shooting contests, the NRA since the late 1970s has devoted most of its resources to defeating gun control legislation in the United States Congress. Its flagship publication is the monthly magazine *American Rifleman*.

Physicians for Social Responsibility
1875 Connecticut Ave., NW, Suite 1012
Washington, DC   20009
(202) 667-4260 • fax: (202) 667-4201
e-mail: psrnatl@psr.org
Web site: www.psr.org

Physicians for Social Responsibility is made up of medical doctors and other health-care professionals who are concerned about the public-health consequences of gun policies. The organization campaigned in 2004 to maintain the federal ban on assault weapons. The group's Web site contains useful fact sheets on firearms and firearm regulations as well as a gun control bibliography.

Second Amendment Foundation (SAF)
12500 NE Tenth Pl., Bellevue, WA   98005
(425) 454-7012 • fax: (425) 451-3959
e-mail: info@saf.org
Web site: www.saf.org

The Second Amendment Foundation defends citizens' rights to privately own and possess firearms. It promotes the view that gun control laws violate this right. SAF maintains biographical archives and a library and publishes the *Journal on Firearms and Public Policy* periodically, the *Second Amendment Reporter* quarterly, *Women and Guns* monthly, and other monographs and pamphlets.

Violence Policy Center
1730 Rhode Island Ave., NW, Suite 1014
Washington, DC   20036
(202) 822-8200
e-mail: info@vpc.org
Web site: www.vpc.org

The Violence Policy Center describes itself as "the most aggressive group in the gun control movement." It engages in education, legislation, and lawsuits in order to further its cause of drastically reducing the number of guns in America. It believes that firearms are a danger to public health and need to be treated like other public menaces. Special reports available from the center's Web site include *Safe at Home: How D.C.'s Gun Laws Save Children's Lives* and *When Men Murder Women: An Analysis of 2003 Homicide Data.*

Women Against Gun Control
PO Box 95357, South Jordan, UT   84095
(801) 328-9660

e-mail: info@wagc.com
Web site: www.wagc.com

An organization dedicated to counteracting the belief that all women support gun control, Women Against Gun Control promotes the view that women's best defense against crime is armed self-defense. Truly a grassroots organization, the group operates a Web site featuring articles on gun safety as well as information on political activism to protect gun rights.

For Further Research

Books

Jervis Anderson, *Guns in American Life*. New York: Random House, 1984.

Marjolijn Bijlefeld, *The Gun Control Debate: A Documentary History*. Westport, CT: Greenwood, 1997.

Sarah Brady and Merrill McLoughlin, *A Good Fight*. New York: Public Affairs, 2002.

Doug Briggs, *A Matter of Personal Protection: Incorporating the Weapons and Self-Defense Laws of Texas*. Spring, TX: Beverly, 1992.

Steven Brill, *Firearm Abuse: A Research and Policy Report*. Washington, DC: Police Foundation, 1977.

Gene Brown, *Violence on America's Streets*. Brookfield, CT: Millbrook, 1992.

Peter H. Brown and Daniel G. Abel, *Outgunned: Up Against the NRA; The First Complete Insider Account of the Battle over Gun Control*. New York: Free Press, 2003.

Gregg Lee Carter, *Gun Control in the United States: A Reference Handbook*. Santa Barbara, CA: ABC-CLIO, 2006.

Robert J. Cottrol, ed., *Gun Control and the Constitution: Sources and Explorations on the Second Amendment*. New York: Garland, 1993.

Cynthia DiLaura Devore, *Kids and Guns*. Edina, MN: Abdo, 1994.

Edward F. Dolan, *Gun Control: A Decision for Americans*. New York: Watts, 1978.

Kelly Doyle, ed., *Is Gun Ownership a Right?* Farmington Hills, MI: Greenhaven, 2005.

Kristin A. Goss, *Disarmed: The Missing Movement for Gun Control in America.* Princeton, NJ: Princeton University Press, 2006.

Bernard E. Harcourt, *Guns, Crime, and Punishment in America.* New York: New York University Press, 2003.

Don B. Kates, *The Great American Gun Debate: Essays on Firearms and Violence.* San Francisco: Pacific Research Institute for Public Policy, 1997.

Caitlin Kelly, *Blown Away: American Women and Guns.* New York: Pocket Books, 2004.

Jens Ludwig and Philip J. Cook, *Evaluating Gun Policy: Effects on Crime and Violence.* Washington, DC: Brookings Institution Press, 2003.

Norman L. Lunger, *Big Bang: The Loud Debate over Gun Control.* Brookfield, CT: Twenty-First Century, 2002.

Richard I. Mack and Timothy Robert Walters, *From My Cold Dead Fingers: Why America Needs Guns.* Safford, AZ: Rawhide Western, 1994.

Joyce Lee Malcolm, *Guns and Violence: The English Experience.* Cambridge, MA: Harvard University Press, 2002.

Eric C. Morgan and David B. Kopel, *The Assault Weapon Panic: "Political Correctness" Takes Aim at the Constitution.* Golden, CO: Independence Institute, 1993.

James M. Murray, *50 Things You Can Do About Guns.* San Francisco: Robert D. Reed, 1994.

Lee Nisbet, *The Gun Control Debate: You Decide.* Buffalo, NY: Prometheus, 1990.

Ted Nugent, *God, Guns and Rock 'n' Roll.* Washington, DC: Regnery, 2000.

Richard Poe, *The Seven Myths of Gun Control: Reclaiming the Truth About Guns, Crime, and the Second Amendment*. Roseville, CA: Forum, 2001.

Robert J. Spitzer, *The Politics of Gun Control*. Washington, DC: CQ Press, 2004.

Helen E. Veit, Kenneth R. Bowling, and Charlene Bangs Bickford, *Creating the Bill of Rights: The Documentary Record from the First Federal Congress*. Baltimore: Johns Hopkins University Press, 1991.

James Q. Wilson and Joan Petersilia, eds., *Crime: Public Policies for Crime Control*. Oakland, CA: ICS Press, 2002.

James D. Wright and Peter Henry Rossi, *The Armed Criminal in America: A Survey of Incarcerated Felons*. Washington, DC: United States Department of Justice, National Institute of Justice, 1985.

Aaron S. Zelman and Richard W. Stevens, *Death by "Gun Control": The Human Cost of Victim Disarmament*. Hartford, WI: Mazel Freedom, 2001.

Franklin E. Zimring and Gordon Hawkins, *The Citizen's Guide to Gun Control*. New York: Macmillan, 1992.

Periodicals

Philip J. Cook and Jens Ludwig, "Fact-Free Gun Policy," *University of Pennsylvania Law Review*, April 1, 2003.

Richard F. Corlin, "The Secrets of Gun Violence in America," *Vital Speeches of the Day*, August 1, 2001.

Michelle Cottle, "Shoot First, Regret Legislation Later: Why Florida's 'Stand Your Ground' Law Is a Bad Idea and One That Could Spread," *Time*, May 9, 2005.

Robert J. Cottrol, "Taking Second Amendment Rights Seriously," *Human Rights*, Fall 1999.

Amy Karan and Helen Stampalia, "Domestic Violence and Firearms: A Deadly Combination: The Juxtaposition of Federal and Florida Laws," *Florida Bar Journal*, October 1, 2005.

Don B. Kates, "Slippery-Slope Gun Control," *Handguns*, October 1, 2005.

Neal Knox, "The History of Gun Politics: Where We Are and How We Got Here," *Hunting*, September 2004.

Abigail A. Kohn, "Straight Shooting on Gun Control," *Reason*, May 2005.

Hugh LaFollette, "Controlling Guns," *Criminal Justice Ethics*, January 2000.

John R. Lott Jr., "Guns, Crime, and Health," *Southern Economic Journal*, July 2000.

———, "Half Cocked: Why Most of What You See in the Media About Guns Is Wrong," *American Enterprise*, July 1, 2003.

Thomas McIntyre, "A Gun Control Update: Restrictions Spread from Handguns to Kitchen Knives," *Sports Afield*, November 1, 2005.

Alice H.G. Phillips, "Living in Different States of Mind: I Hate Guns; My Boyfriend Sells Them for a Living. Will We Still Be Standing When the Smoke Clears?" *Newsweek*, January 26, 2004.

Steven Riczo, "Guns, America, and the 21st Century," *USA Today* magazine, March 2001.

Richard Rosenfeld, "The Limits of Crime Control," *Journal of Criminal Law and Criminology*, Autumn 2002.

Tom W. Smith, "Public Opinion About Gun Policies," *Future of Children*, Summer/Autumn 2002.

Cynthia A. Stark, "Fundamental Rights and the Right to Bear Arms," *Criminal Justice Ethics*, Winter/Spring 2001.

Lisa Stein, "Under the Gun," *U.S. News & World Report*, September 20, 2004.

Lance K. Stell, "Gun Control and the Regulation of Fundamental Rights," *Criminal Justice Ethics*, Winter/Spring, 2001.

————, "The Production of Criminal Violence in America: Is Strict Gun Control the Solution?" *Journal of Law, Medicine and Ethics*, March 22, 2004.

Dana Sullivan, "Straight Talk About Guns: Safety Report: What You Need to Teach Your Child—Even If You Don't Own a Gun," *Parenting*, May 1, 2004.

Index